S0-BZW-507

BATTLE
OF THE BULGE

0 11557 01352 8

The Stackpole Military History Series

BATTLE OF THE BULGE

Volume Three:
The 3rd Fallschirmjäger Division in
Action, December 1944–January 1945

Hans Wijers

STACKPOLE
BOOKS

Copyright © 2014 by Hans Wijers

Published by
STACKPOLE BOOKS
5067 Ritter Road
Mechanicsburg, PA 17055
www.stackpolebooks.com

All rights reserved, including the right to reproduce this book or portions
thereof in any form or by any means, electronic or mechanical, including
photocopying, recording, or by any information storage and retrieval
system, without permission in writing from the publisher. All inquiries
should be addressed to Stackpole Books.

Printed in the United States of America

10 9 8 7 6 5 4 3 2 1

Cover design by Wendy A. Reynolds

The Library of Congress has cataloged the first volume as follows:

Wijers, Hans J.
  The Battle of the Bulge / Hans Wijers.
    v. cm. — (Stackpole military history series)
  Includes index.
  Contents: v. 1. The Losheim Gap/Holding the line.
  ISBN 978-0-8117-3592-6
  1. Ardennes, Battle of the, 1944–1945. I. Title.
  D756.5.A7W55 2009
  940.54'219348—dc22
                        2009011932

ISBN 978-0-8117-1352-8

To my father, Jan Wijers (1925–1989)

I miss you every day, pa. You're looking down on me from a faraway world, but one day we will be reunited. I remember what you told me when I was a young boy, and I can now better understand what you didn't tell me but I could see in your eyes. Thanks for the great moments we had together—they made me who I am today.

Contents

Foreword

This book by Hans Wijers describes more than just the battles that took place in the Ardennes from 16 December 1944 until the end of January 1945. It tells of the conflict between two opposing armies in the northern shoulder of the Ardennes in Belgium and revolves around the men who served their countries in this pitched engagement. These men were not household names such as Dwight Eisenhower, George Patton, Gerd von Rundstedt, and Sepp Dietrich, generals in command during this horrendous battle in the Ardennes in 1944–45, but they were heroes in every sense of the word. They fought valiantly for their countries.

As I write this on a cold winter day in Powhatan, Virginia, I think about the cold and deep snow in the Ardennes and what these soldiers were going through. The pictures and graphics help to relay the extreme conditions that the soldiers experienced. American and German soldiers were locked in mortal combat during the most festive holiday season, Christmas, a time of rejoicing, merriment, and, of course, family. Letters and thoughts of these young men, both American and German, turn to their God, family, and comrades in arms. The author has a unique gift for taking documents, pictures, personal thoughts, and private letters and weaving them into a mosaic about the Battle of the Bulge.

Hans is a historian in every sense of the word. He has once again been able to capture and place into words the life of these soldiers and what they experienced in this battle in December 1944 and January 1945. It is a gift to be able to have these men's thoughts come alive on paper and offer a true account of the Battle of the Bulge in the northern shoulder. By gaining the trust and respect of living American and German soldiers and the families of soldiers who lost their lives in the Ardennes in 1944 and 1945, Hans gives the reader an accurate picture of the unbelievable endurance of the soldiers during the most extreme conditions.

I also think about my father, *Hauptmann* Heinz Fick of the 2nd Company, 1st Battalion, *Fallschirmjäger-Regiment 9, 3rd Fallschirmjäger-Division,* who fell in Amel on 20 January 1945 and now lies in his eternal rest in the German soldiers' cemetery in Recogne-Bastogne with nearly 7,000 other German soldiers. A visit to the American cemetery at Henri-Chapelle took my breath away; it was impressive to see the 7,800 white crosses of the Americans buried with their comrades in this truly beautiful setting in the Ardennes. I make reference to these cemeteries because this story has brought home to me the utter senselessness of this battle. The pictures and words in this book are about men who gave their lives and futures for their countries. An individual can do no more for country and family.

Hans, my friend, thanks for taking the time to put this book together so that the men who fought and some who gave their lives will be forever remembered in history. I also feel that other family members, like me, whose loved ones fell in the Battle of the Bulge, will get a true sense of what these men endured. May God be with all those American and German soldiers who have told their story so that generations can remember those who fought in this epic conflict.

Heinrich A. Gideons

CHAPTER 1

The *3rd Fallschirmjäger Division*

Commanded by *Generalmajor* Walter Wadehn, the *3rd Fallschirmjäger-Division* was hastily rebuilt in the Netherlands from battered remnants of the division that had escaped from France. It was mainly filled up with excess *Luftwaffe* personnel, and both men and officers were woefully inexperienced. In November *OB-West* committed the division near Aachen, where it encountered the American drive through the northeastern fringes of the Hürtgenwald.

Although the *Fallschirmjäger* succeeded in stopping the American drive, they paid dearly for their inexperience. As the target date for the offensive approached, the division was still locked in bitter fighting near Düren, and it proved almost impossible to extricate it.

On 10 December 1944, only one regiment, *Fallschirmjäger-Regiment 9*, had been relieved by the fully re-organized and equipped *47th Volksgrenadier Division*.

The combat strength of *Fallschirmjäger-Regiment 9* had been considerably diminished by the previous fighting. The three battalions that constituted the regiment had an average strength of only 1,200 men. *Fallschirmjäger-Regiment 5* and *Fallschirmjäger-Regiment 8* were relieved in parts on 13 and 14 December 1944. Both regiments were exhausted and had taken a severe beating. On 14 December 1944, after forced night marches, the first units of the *3rd Fallschirmjäger Division* arrived in the assigned assembly area at Schüller, a village near the town of Stadkyll. Upon release of the division, the Fifteenth Army reported that they were incapable of any offensive action, at least for some days.

1

In an effort to transfer the troops of the division as quickly as possible to the zone of attack, part of one regiment was hastily loaded into lorries borrowed from *1st SS-Panzerkorps* and, while leaving its heavy infantry weapons behind, transported to the concentration zone. The other elements, including the heavy infantry weapons, were to move on foot to the assigned zone, where they arrived in the evening of 16 December 1944, too late to take part in the initial phase of the offensive. Personnel strength of the *3rd Fallschirmjäger-Division* was estimated at approximately 75 percent of authorization. The division lacked the support of self-propelled guns.

Hauptmann Heinz Fick, company commander in the 2nd Battalion of *Fallschirmjäger-Regiment 9,* wrote in a letter to his wife: "West front, 12 December 1944. I just started to write a letter to my mother, as we got the order to move out. During the following night, we left our positions. Luckily, without any losses, because the American artillery was constantly bombarding us. That is now three days ago. In the meantime we have more than sixty kilometers behind us. The men have to carry a lot, and all look very exhausted. We moved to the south and are now in the Eifel area. Here it is already winter: snow, frost, icy roads. The men are not even equipped with good winter clothes—I feel sorry for them, as we received hardly anything of the winter clothing that was promised."

The *3rd Fallschirmjäger-Division,* forming the left wing in the initial disposition for the attack, had a zone of advance roughly following the southern shoulder of the road to Honsfeld (*Rollbahn D,* or D route).

The division went into combat with two groups: on the right, *Fallschirmjäger-Regiment 9* moving via Berterath–Lanzerath–Honsfeld–Hepscheid toward Schoppen; and on the left, *Fallschirmjäger-Regiment 8* moving via Krewinkel–Manderfeld–Holzheim–Wereth toward Eibertingen. The area selected for the breakthrough attempt comprised the northern half of the U.S. 14th Cavalry Group's sector and took in most of the gap between the cavalry and the U.S. 99th Infantry Division to its north.

In the first hours of the advance, then, the *3rd Fallschirmjäger-Division* would be striking against the 14th Cavalry Group in the Krewinkel–Berterath area. But the final objective of the division's attack was ten miles to the northwest, the line Schoppen–Eibertingen on Route D. The division's axis thus extended through the right of the U.S. 99th Infantry Division.

Fick wrote in a letter to his wife on 14 December: "Since yesterday afternoon, after several days of marching through small towns and little roads on foot, we came to our new positions. The men are happy that they finally get some rest, and next to that finally can also warm them up in a pre-heated house, even if it is just a small place. Shoes, clothes, even the weapons all have to be fixed and re-checked. Even the body needs a good washing. So the little time we have will be used to the last minute . . .

"At this moment we are located in a little village in the Eifel. The people here are very friendly to us. They are very poor, but they share what they have with us; we get soup and bread. We are ready for our new assignment, and how tough it will be, because not only the enemy will be putting up a stiff defense, but also the terrain and the winter will make it hard for us, but we all believe that we will succeed."

When the *3rd Fallschirmjäger-Division* went into battle, it had severe losses on its first days against elements of the 99th Infantry Division, which put up a stiff fight to delay the German advance.

CHAPTER 2

The Battle for Lanzerath, 16 December 1944

Lanzerath was defended by the I&R (Intelligence and Reconnaissance) Platoon of the 394th Infantry Regiment of the U.S. 99th Infantry Division and was attacked by *Fallschirmjäger-Regiment 9* of the *3rd Fallschirmjäger-Division.*

Oberschütze Rudi Frühbeisser, *Fallschirmjäger-Regiment 9, 3rd Fallschirmjäger-Division,* wrote an account of this costly attack on the defense positions at Lanzerath. It shows how hard his unit was hit by the defenders of the hilltop looking over the road Lanzerath–Honsfeld: "Six o'clock! All of a sudden this hellish spectacle stops! There is the order: 'Attack!' We go in at the double! Suddenly, the enemy territory in front of us is bathed in a milky-white light. Hundreds of searchlights are used to create an artificial moonlight. The company is advancing steadily. We old men have been continually waiting for it. Now it should begin! All of a sudden, we reach a road that is at right angles to us. One man shouts that this is the road which forms the Belgian border. We continue to advance, pass another small road, and close in on a height. We reach the small hamlet of Hergersberg. To our right, in front of us, tank engines are roaring on a road. Now we have reached the main road. To our right, the large Belgian customs house is standing by the side of the street. Where the road twists its way down into a valley, there is a big explosion in front of us. To the side of the road, a tank has run over a mine (laid by the German troops when they where retreating earlier).

"So the road that forks off to the right and which we'll have to take is mined. Now we can use the break and study the map

Rudi Frühbeisser.

with the chief. So now we are lying by the road that is coming from Losheimergraben and is leading towards Manderfeld. Our first objective should be the small village of Hüllscheid, which is lying on the hill slope behind a mill. Slowly, dawn creeps up. A squad of Kuhlbach's platoon advances on the road to provide cover. We see no Yanks. Now we have passed the mill, after a signal has come in from forward troops. To our right the road from Losheimergraben is coming down. So forward on our left. By a row of high firs we proceed with caution. Suddenly, a heavy machine gun opens up!"

Mortar fire rained down on the village. *Fahnenjunker-Oberjäger* Herbert Vogt, who was hunkering down next to

Frühbeisser, was shot in the neck. Frühbeisser quickly dragged him into the house opposite. The round must have gone straight through the throat, thought Frühbeisser, who already had some experience in the matter. *Bang!* An antitank gun must have shot straight through the house. Rubble and stones flew through the air. Squad leader Lassek was mortally wounded. The sergeant-medic of the 1st Company was also killed. Captain Schiffke, the 1st Company commander, sent some men into the foremost house, as there was a better view from there. They spotted a Yank up in a big tree in the woods. *Boom!* A rifle grenade fired at him, and the Yank tumbled out of the tree.

The 2nd Battalion attacked the village of Merlscheid from Backelsberg, which lay behind Hüllscheid. Again and again one could hear the high barking of an antitank gun firing into the village. According to the map, it should have been higher up at the crossroads, which on the right runs toward Lanzerath and on the left toward Hasenvenn. After a while, the men succeeded in making their way forward and found the signalers with their radios lying by the side of the road. They belong to the signals platoon of the 2nd Battalion. Five of them have been killed; the others, severely wounded. Here the runner of the staff of the 1st Battalion, *Gefreiter* Peter Heidkamp, got it in his right hand. However, he passed his orders on to the company commander. *Stabsfeldwebel* Schega of the 1st Company with his squad managed to break through a wall into a house. From there they knocked out an American machine gun. They continued and, after a few shots, reached Merlscheid safely.

"Yanks really must have lived here," Frühbeisser said. "Food stands around on tables everywhere. American weapons, ammunition, and equipment are captured by us. The first American cigarettes are smoked in this battle. A squad from the 15th Company, which is located in a house in Hüllscheid, takes a direct hit. *Oberschütze* Mittelmann, *Obergefreiter* Hermann, *Gefreiter* Conrad, *Gefreiter* Wittig, and *Gefreiter* Pfau are killed straightaway. *Schütze* Eder is killed by a shell from an infantry gun. In Merlscheid, *Schütze* Hildebrand of the

Modern view of Lanzerath. The village consisted of twenty-
three houses and a church. A tall fir forest enclosed the
village on two sides. Here a fierce fight took place with the
weak American forces who remained.

14th company, shot through the head by an infantry gun, is
killed outright. The 2nd Battalion now has crossed the road
leading to Lanzerath. The 1st Battalion from Merlscheid is
approaching Lanzerath via a small road."

Snow covered the field to the front of the I&R Platoon of
the 394th Infantry Regiment (99th Infantry Division) and
extended 200 yards down to the first house in Lanzerath. The
field was bisected by a farm fence about four feet high, creating a main line of resistance. The two- and three-man foxhole
bunkers were covered with six- to eight-inch pine logs. The
interlocking fields of fire created a final protective line meas-
uring up to Fort Benning's "school solution." The .50-caliber
machine gun mounted on the jeep was in a defilade position.
Fresh snow had fallen several times and camouflaged the position beyond detection. A bitter cold had temperatures ranging
from the teens at night to the twenties and low thirties during
the day. Snow was two to four inches deep in the fields and
drifting. The sharp wind gusted from the north and forced a
freezing fog to roll into and out of the platoon area.

Lieutenant Warren Springer of the 371st Field Artillery, 99th Infantry Division, wrote: "On the fifteenth of December 1944, Peter Gacki, Willard Wibben, Billy Queen, and I were in a house on the east side of the road in Lanzerath that served as our base and observation post. I don't remember anyone else being in the house on that day or the next. On the second floor of the house, there was a window that provided a good view of Losheim and the Schnee Eiffel area. Sandbags were in place against the wall just below the level of the window ledge. A BC scope was in place to aid in observation of the enemy area. During the morning on the fifteenth, we spotted a man riding into Lanzerath on a bicycle. I questioned him, and he said he had come into the village to pick up some shoes he had left with a cousin so that they could be repaired. Somehow his story didn't seem quite right, so I took him to a building diagonally across the street where there were a number of our troops. I don't remember if they were part of the tank destroyer group or some of the I&R Platoon. I wanted to see if any of them had seen the suspect around before. As I remember, the person in charge of the group said he would have a couple of his men take the suspect back to Battalion S-2 for questioning."

Lieutenant Lyle Bouck Jr., commander of the I&R Platoon, 394th Infantry Regiment, 99th Infantry Division, recalled: "Suddenly, without warning, a barrage of artillery registered at about 0500 hours and continued until about 0700 hours. The artillery was relentless and frightening, but not devastating. Much landed short, wide, and long of our position, and mostly tree bursts. At any rate, our well-protected cover prevented casualties. The telephone lines were out, but the one radio allowed us to report to the regiment. Kriz told us that regiment and the entire front had received the same artillery. He suggested some forward patrol action, and to maintain contact. As a patrol was being prepared, three jeeps and several trucks (the 801st Tank Destroyer Unit in Lanzerath) came up the road, turned left at the platoon left flank, and headed for Buchholz Station. This information was reported to regiment.

Lyle Bouck.

First Lt. Ed Buenger (394th assistant S-2) explained this to Kriz and Riley. We were directed to get someone into the village and try to determine what was happening. Slape and Creger went into Lanzerath and occupied the command post vacated by the tank destroyers. As Slape went forward, he took a field phone; he and Creger ran a new wire for contact.

"The next hour or so, nothing happened. Then Slape reported what appeared to be a column of troops marching toward Lanzerath. This was reported to regiment, and I asked permission to withdraw and engage in a delaying action. Kriz said to remain in position and some reinforcements would come from the 3rd Battalion. Slape called again and said some Germans were in the house (downstairs) and he and Creger wanted help. I sent McGhee, Silvola, and Robinson across the road, told them to creep along the ditch, get close to the second house on the left, open fire, and see if they could release Slape and Creger. Sak went forward to the point foxhole and Fort monitored the radio. In the meantime, Slape and Creger slipped out of the house, into a barn, under some cows, and out the other side, into the woods. While they circled north in the draw and woods, McGehee, Silvola, and Robinson closed into the village and engaged in a fire fight and wiped out what they described as platoon in size. At this time, Sak reported seeing a young girl come out of the corner house, on the right, and talk to the German soldiers, pointing north. When this happened, Risto Milosevich and I crept out the rear of the platoon position, crossed the road to Buchholz and entered a group of sapling pines (about five to six feet tall) in hopes of locating or learning something of Slape, Creger, McGehee, Silvola, Robinson. The entire platoon was firing for a short time. Then, suddenly, Slape and Creger appeared in the small trees with Risto and me. Slape was crouched forward and moaning; he told of falling as he slipped while running across the road (from Lanzerath to Losheimergraben). As he ran following Creger, the Germans fired upon him with an automatic weapon, and shot the heel of his shoe off. Later, we learned he had fractured two ribs in the incident, which caused him pain."

Rudi Frühbeisser of *Fallschirmjäger-Regiment 9* continues his story: "A loud single explosion. Captain Schiffke has been hit in his arm. A *Stabsfeldwebel* medic quickly bandages his chief. He got a grazing wound on the upper arm. Now the 1st, 2nd, and 3rd Companies have run into opposition. Weapons specialist Federowski is hit. And Willi Kölker also is wounded by a round in the upper thigh. Bradel from Vienna is killed. The 2nd Battalion also has got engaged in combat. There the commander of the 6th Company, *Hauptmann* Theetz, falls. A machine-gun crew consisting of Hoffmann, Ollermann, and Jähring all are mortally hit by headshots while lying at their gun. Platoon commander Otto Pleie, a veteran of Normandy, takes a round in the shoulder. Within the 4th Company of *Oberleutnant* Grau, platoon commander Ilk and Weishäupel are hit. The tank killer squad leader, Klein, and Noak both fall with head shots."

Lyle Bouck continues: "The four of us crept across Buchholz road and back into the rear of the platoon position. All of this movement was accomplished without exposure, because we were below the crest of the hill. Slape was not aware of McGhee's fate. McGehee, Silvola, and Robinson all described later how they were cut off from the platoon and traveled north to reach the 1st Battalion to try to get some help (not knowing help would not come, as all units were having the same problems as we). In their movement north, they had to negotiate the deep RR cut (thirty to forty feet deep) containing the tracks running from Losheim to Buchholz Station. At this time, they were in another fire fight with a battalion of German troops wearing 'white' to blend in with the snow. Robinson was badly wounded, the calf of his right leg was ripped open. Silvola was wounded severely in the left elbow. They were trapped on the north bank of the RR cut and captured at gun point. I told Slape and Creger to get into McGhee's vacated hole. As they crept forward to do so, the first attack by the Germans was made on our position. This may have been two platoons, storming up the snow covered slope, trying to get over a fence to our position."

Rudi Frühbeisser resumes his account: "The 2nd Company is carrying out a storming attack on a small section of wood 300 meters left of the street. During the attack, platoon commander Karl Quator and Fischer, as well as Rench and Roth and Heube are killed. Platoon commander P (?) is wounded. The 1st Company cannot proceed. The fir forest is strongly mined. Some now try to clear the mines. Our old *Oberschütze* Winter, who was in Russia with *General* Meindl, is slightly wounded in his arm. Winter is a *Gau* orator in the NSDAP. One man jokingly teases him, 'So, Hans, you with your golden party membership badge are impervious to more than a scratch.' And, as if he really is invulnerable, he walks back to the street in order to get bandaged by the medic, Otto."

Lyle Bouck again: "The attack was repelled and this action reported to regiment. Somewhere during this time, three strangers joined us. They came in a jeep. One was a first lieutenant forward observer and two of his men. (Seems he was part of the tank destroyer unit.)*"

Lt. Warren Springer of 371st Field Artillery Battalion, 99th Infantry Division, remembers: "Although there had been some increase in activity both during the day and night in the area

---

*Actually the 371st Field Artillery Battalion.

around Losheim before 16 December, it hardly prepared us for the intensity of the enemy artillery barrage that opened up around 0530 that morning. This continued for more than an hour. The area in front of our observation post was blackened by a concentration of artillery shells that had fallen short by about fifty yards. The concentrated pattern made it clear that the enemy knew that the house was used as an observation post. I remembered the man we had questioned the previous day and suspected that he or someone else had passed on information on our location.

"When the barrage lifted, we watched from our window for signs of enemy approaching, but none appeared. I went outside to check the road and saw the tank destroyer group pulling out. I stopped one of the vehicles and was told a strong German force was advancing up the road. I called the Fire Direction Center, told them of the situation, and asked for artillery fire on the road 200 yards south of our post. They told me they could not do anything at that time because they were under small-arms attack. A short time later, two or three men appeared in a jeep and said they were on their way to a prepared defense position and advised us to go with them since the Germans were right behind them. I was glad that artillery fire had not been delivered when I requested it because these men might have been casualties. I had been under the impression from the tank destroyer group that they were the last ones out. We followed the men a short distance north on the Lanzerath road, turned left and followed a trail up to the prepared position. There were several foxholes, or dugouts, in the area. Each one was surrounded and covered with logs and dirt. There were narrow openings in front for firing and an entrance in back. The I&R Platoon, commanded by Lieutenant Bouck, was already in place. Bouck, or one of his men, directed Gacki, Wibben, and me to one of the dugouts and asked Billy Queen to join two or three of his men in one of the other dugouts. I think these men were the same ones who led us to the position.

"Lieutenant Bouck asked me if I could bring in some artillery fire. I told him I would try, but they were under attack back in the rear area and might not be able to respond. I did get through on the radio and asked for artillery fire in front of our position. I was told they would try to give us artillery support as soon as possible, but reinforcements were out of the question. A short time later, some rounds came in to our right front. I asked for a correction to bring the fire directly in front of the position and also asked that they drop some fire on the Lanzerath road in the vicinity of our observation post in the house we had occupied to prevent enemy reinforcements, particularly armored vehicles, from coming from that direction.

"A few more rounds came in, but they were still too far to the right, and I asked for a further correction. Just then there was a loud crash just in back of our dugout and the noise of shattered glass. At that point my radio went dead. I don't know if it was a mortar shell or machine-gun fire that hit our jeep, but I knew that was the end of communication with our firing batteries.

"No further artillery fire landed in our immediate area. I thought I heard artillery fire landing at the other location where I had requested fire, namely down the Lanzerath road about 200 yards from the house we had used as an observation post. I cautiously stuck my head and shoulders out of the entrance on the rear aspect of our dugout to see where the shells were landing, but I could only judge from the sound because my vision in that direction was obstructed. At that point some twigs started dropping from an overhanging tree branch just in back of our dugout. I realized the twigs were being clipped off by bullets, so like a turtle, I quickly pulled back into the dugout.

"I waited for more artillery fire to be dropped in our area, but that didn't happen. When our radio communication was interrupted so abruptly, back at fire direction center they may have thought that we had been captured and would be exposed to any fire landing in our area."

The 3rd Company of Captain Woitschek stopped in the left part of the village.

Rudi Frühbeisser of *Fallschirmjäger-Regiment 9* continues: "Here there is snow lying on the heights and so the paratroopers in their mottled smocks really stand out. When the 3rd Company continues to close with the houses, platoon commander Schiele stumbles and does not get up anymore. When somebody turns him over, he concludes, 'Headshot!' Mayer and Schmidt have been wounded less severely. The call 'Medic!' goes out. Medic Matthieu walks to the wounded. He is clearly recognizable with the red cross on his chest. A red cross flag hangs from his back pack on a metal rod. Suddenly, as he is treating the wounded, there is a shot; he grasps his face and keels over. Headshot! Then medic Schmidt runs out to help— he also is hit by a headshot!"

Lieutenant Bouck continues: "Sometime in mid-afternoon, a second attack was made and repelled, but it left its mark on the I&R Platoon. While I was giving information to Lieutenant Buenger on the radio during a lull, small-arms fire from a sniper shot the transmitter out of my hand. I was not wounded. Kalil was struck in the face with a rifle grenade that failed to detonate. As the grenade fell to the floor of the foxhole, Kalil was stunned. His face was lacerated, his jaw and cheekbone fractured, his teeth imbedded into the roof of his mouth. Redmond used two first-aid kits and bandaged Kalil in an expert manner. About this time, the Germans presented a 'white' flag and another with a 'red-cross,' indicating a desire to tend to their wounded. While they were accomplishing this, Milosevich detected a helper leaning over a wounded soldier and appeared to be talking into a communications device. Soon mortar fire landed behind our location; a few rounds fell short. At this time, Milosevich put the 'imposter' out of action.

"The communications were out, ammunition was running low, the wounded increasing, and apprehension running high. I told Sak to get Slape, Dustman, and Redmond. Our evaluation was not impressive. We realized heavy fighting was taking place north of us at 1st Battalion and to the northwest where 3rd Battalion was in reserve at Buchholz Station. (Later, of course, we learned it was the German *12th Volksgrenadier-Division* battling the 1st Battalion and the same unit reaching

Buchholz Station by way of the railroad cut.) This meant we were cut off and could only retreat on foot. I told Slape to send Jenkins and Preston back to regiment or 3rd Battalion to tell them our problem, and that we would hold as long as possible. Also that we planned to withdraw under the cover of darkness and, if possible, get some help. Jenkins and Preston made it back to regiment, but not until the eighteenth of December. The headquarters was no longer in Hünningen, having to withdraw to Elsenborn. Jenkins and Preston, out of ammunition, were captured the following day at the point of a bayonet in a hayloft. A third attack was directed on the platoon later in the afternoon; this was also repelled. During this attack, Sak jumped up on the jeep and was firing the .50 caliber until I told him to get down and take cover. Moments later, Slape manned the .50 caliber and was firing when automatic enemy fire hit the breech and rendered the machine gun inoperable. As dusk approached, thoughts were directed toward getting out on foot, leaving the foxholes that had offered security to us for the entire day. Our ammo was not out, but it was low.

"All of a sudden, and no one knows from what direction, our entire platoon was infiltrated by Germans. Some firing, screaming, and running. Sak, who earlier had been firing the .50-caliber machine gun on the jeep, leaned out of the rear of our emplacement and emptied his last clip of ammo at three Germans running toward the foxhole vacated by Jenkins and Preston. I leaned out for a moment and unloaded by last full extended clip at two Germans about twenty yards away. As I ducked back into the hole, automatic small-arms fire ripped into our emplacement. Sak and I were now helpless, sure we had been located by the Germans. Just then, the end of a burp-gun barrel pointed into our hole. As I leaned to the right, I pushed Sak to the left. A burst of five or six rounds exploded, and Sak slumped to the floor of the foxhole. I found myself reaching down to help him; as I did, I was aware that I was being aided by two Germans lifting Sak. We got him out of the hole, the growing dusk made vision limited, but the severity of

Vince Kuhlbach.

Sak's wounding was evident when the Germans shined a flash-light on him. He had been struck along the right side of his face. Everything from the right side of his nose to his right ear was missing. His right eyeball hanging from the socket.

"At this time, everything seemed quiet, with small amounts of sporadic rifle fire. A voice asked calmly, 'Who is the com-mandant?' I informed him it was me. He wanted to know what my men were going to do. I told him I would call them from their positions if he would have his men stop firing. This was accomplished, and we were searched. (I later met this man, when, in 1969, survivors of the campaign met in Lanzerath to commemorate the twenty-fifth anniversary of the battle. His

name is Vince Kuhlbach, a CPA in Cologne.) Then I was told
to help two German guards escort Sak down the hill. As we
walked around and over bodies, one guard stopped us and
wanted to know if we had been at St. Lô. I told him, 'Nein,'
and he muttered something like 'Mein Kamaraden.'

"We were taken into a small café in Lanzerath and placed
on a bench just inside and to the right of the door. Others in
the I&R Platoon were ordered to help carry German wounded
into the village. As Sak sat on my left side (seeming to pass out
and come to), I wondered how long he could last (due to the
severity of the wound and the constant blood loss). The paper
bandages used by the Germans were poor by our standards.
Kalil was brought in. Redmond's wound wrapping was excellent (so well, I didn't know who he was). I could only see his
nose and one eye. Slape, Milosevich, and I discussed the possibility of breaking out the back door (during the confusion in
the room). We agreed we could never bring Sak and Kalil with
us, so the decision was to stay.

"Activity increased as the night passed. Shortly after a clock
on the wall struck 'midnight,' considerable excitement took
place. A group of *Panzer* officers stormed into the café, making
demands and issuing lengthy orders. They placed a map
against a wall by sticking two bayonets into the map. With light
of lanterns they pointed, talked, screamed and stalked about
as different officers came into and out of the room. The rum-
ble and churn of tanks could be heard through the remainder
of the night. Artillery fell in the area through the night, but
none hit the café. As dawn approached, I was instructed to
place Sak on the floor with the other wounded. He still had his
wallet and a small Bible. I removed a picture of his girlfriend
(Chloe) from his wallet, placed the picture and the Bible on
his chest, and said a few words of prayer, and told him I
pledged that we would see each other back in the States. I told
him we were being separated now, and I placed the picture
back in his wallet and put it and his Bible in his field jacket
pocket, and said, 'Good-bye.' He could not speak, but I am
certain he heard me, because he squeezed my hand."

Sergeant Peter Gacki recalls: "After we had been searched, Wibben and I had to help carry a wounded German back to Lanzerath. We later learned that Cpl. Billy Queen, who had gone to another foxhole, had been wounded and died (in January, Cleon Janos, a member of another C Battery forward observer party, found the body of Billy Queen where he had died earlier). Queen was the only one of the eighteen men that died in that battle. We were kept at Lanzerath that night, then began our journey to a POW camp."

Back to Rudi Frühbeisser of *Fallschirmjäger-Regiment 9*: "With this, the battle for Lanzerath has come to an end. At the 2nd Battalion, where the fight flares up once again, seven men are killed. According to the map, we are stuck in the Büllinger Forest. In front of us, the roads forks. On the right it leads to Losheimergraben; on the left it leads to the small railway station of Buchholz. One guy jokingly says that the commander of the 3rd Battalion, Buchholz, has taken his own railway station with him for good measure. Until dusk we remain lying at the edge of the woods. Opposite the street to our right, there is a small plantation of young fir trees. Well, there could be a surprise lying in wait for us there. With five men and Sergeant Kuhlbach we manage to cross the street. When nothing happens, the entire company follows. Spread out, we continue. As precaution, everyone is walking in the ditches on both sides of the street, which at this point is a sort of drainage ditch and therefore is deep.

"The rising full moon shines brightly. The company is getting forward well. After a kilometer, a fork to the right between the fir trees in the snow can be made out. According to the map, it should be the road leading to the station. All of a sudden, we take fire from a wood to our right. It is a good thing that we all were in the ditch and that probably only our heads were visible. Bright red, the explosive bullets howl over our heads. The machine gun is less than ten meters in front of us. A hand grenade would be useless in the thick forest. So we all turn about, and as well as possible, we hasten back. After about a hundred meters, everybody crosses to the other side of the street. In a lightly planted wood, we remain lying down. Immediately, our machine guns take up position, and a small front is established. Everyone remains lying in a covering position. Now we learn that squad leader Lenz is missing. No one is able to say where he has gone. Some want to walk back the same road again to look for him, but the chief forbids it. Some say that when the machine gun opened up, Lenz had jumped into the woods. Following orders, the company then has to withdraw to Lanzerath. In the first four houses, the paratroopers make themselves as comfortable as possible. Sentries are posted, and the houses are secured. After about two hours, a sentry comes rushing into the cellar and shouts: '*Hauptmann*, there is a shape crawling toward us in the roadside ditch!' Immediately, Kuhlbach and three men are sent out. Correct: there is a shape creeping towards the houses very slowly.

"'We'll capture him,' the sergeant says. Now we see in the moonlight that the shape is one of our paratroopers. Great is our joy when we see that it is the missing Karl Lenz. In the cellar, Lenz reports, 'When the machine gun opened up, it only took me a few jumps to be into the woods. The firing flashes made it easy for me to make out its location exactly. I remained standing behind a thick tree and observed. When the gun finally stopped firing, I noticed to my horror that I was alone in the woods. A few steps in front of me, I could hear the Yanks whisper. I also understood something that sounded like 'dead man.' So they thought I had been killed. After a while, both Americans left their pit. I was determined to sell my skin as expensively as possible. My finger already was on the trigger of my submachine gun. But suddenly both Yanks retreated into the forest. I waited a bit more and then ran as quickly as possible back to the street and continued in the ditch. Now I didn't know where the company had gone. Suddenly, I noticed a large number of footprints which had crossed the street in the snow. So the company had withdrawn. Then I crawled on until I reached Lanzerath.'

"The company commander also is happy that everything has turned out so well. According to a report from battalion staff, we had captured eight men from the U.S. 14th Cavalry Group, a large amount of war booty, including several jeeps. The losses in the battalion are supposed to be sixteen killed, sixty-three wounded, and thirteen missing! The night is quiet."

CHAPTER 3

Honsfeld Is Taken by Surprise

Honsfeld was the rest center of the 99th Infantry Division and was occupied by a variety of troops. A USO show with Marlene Dietrich was supposed to take place on 16 December 1944, but instead Sepp Dietrich and parts of his 6th Panzer Army came.

Private First Class Rex Whitehead of H Company, 394th Infantry Regiment, 99th Infantry Division, remembers: "On 15 December 1944, I was sniffed out by someone in charge of sending men 'back' to have a shower. Have never put this in print before, but I was a bit miffed (pardon the army slang) to have been chosen, for I had a shower just before we left England about November 3 when the order came down to wear jockey longs. It was not the first time someone had pulled 'rank' on me, and I felt they were unjustified. After all, the weather had been cool, and in Idaho the mothers during this season 'sewed' their kid into long johns. (Some of you may have missed the 'rank' bit of Idaho humor used.)

"Now, moving along, I left the positions we had in Germany and went a few hundred yards west to Belgium with guys with strange names like Fleck, Waters, Foley, Boocher, and Smith to a small village of Honsfeld, which had been named 'Camp Maxey.' It had a portable shower setup we were to use. Plus, Foley and Boocher were to stay an extra day, because their feet looked like trench feet should—bad. The shower would not work that evening, but they did give us a change of clothes, which helped somewhat. I have tried that trick since, and it still does not work real well. But, we did get to sleep in a building for the first time in over a month, and a movie was shown. The sound did not work, which surprised no one, and did not

23

matter for those present supplied the words, and would guess they were funnier than the real ones. At least 'dirtier.'

"I slept on a table in the Rec Hall, for there was no room on the floor. That was after a good chat with Smitty the Medic, who had become my friend in the barracks at Maxey, but now with the machine gun platoons. Early the next morning, there was a loud noise, reported as a buzz bomb that had been shot down, and some shingles were lost from the roof. I think it was artillery after all the study of the Bulge, but really does not matter—at least as to which side's artillery.

"The next morning, rumors said 'something' was going on at the front (three miles east), and they even told all the medics to assemble to leave, including Smitty. We were scheduled to leave in the morning, but hoped that whatever was going on would continue, for Marlene Dietrich would be at the Rec Hall about noon to present a program. As the day wore on, it was a typical army day, with nuthin' going on until afternoon when rumors said things were happening, such as Marlene would not be there, and the trucks we were to go back in were delayed. They appeared just before dark, and by that time we were aware things were screwed up, but that surprised no one - with or without trench foot. When we got on the trucks, Foley and Boocher, who had another day of rear area living promised, debated what to do, for the stories were things were 'not good.' They decided to stay their promised one-more-day, for 'What the hell—we can walk back tomorrow if we have to.' It was dark as we left on the trucks, and those two guys were captured before daylight the next morning. The rest of us went back to the front line positions where it was safe. I have made good decisions all my life—before and after that day in Honsfeld."

Two platoons of the 801st Tank Destroyer Battalion had been sent in by General Lauer to Honsfeld to hold the road. Every platoon consisted of three towed 3-inch antitank guns. They were placed just outside Honsfeld. Two protected the road from Lanzerath coming in to Honsfeld, and one pro-tected the road that came from Holzheim. During the night a few towed guns from the 612th Tank Destroyer Battalion were added to the defenses.

Rex Whitehead.

At approximately 2100 hours onf 16 December, B Company of the 612th Tank Destroyer Battalion was alerted for movement by the 23rd Infantry Regiment and told to be prepared to move on the road to Büllingen. They arrived at the initial point during the night. Here they spent an hour before a messenger came from 23rd Infantry Regiment stating the company would move on the road to Büllingen. While en route, the company commander received conflicting orders from 23rd Regimental Combat Team. The first order stated that B Company was to report to an engineer officer in Büllingen. The second order received by a messenger a few minutes later stated that he would report to a tank destroyer officer instead. This certainly was confusing, but the company continued to move as ordered along the designated route. The vigorous reconnaissance previously conducted by the company paid dividends, otherwise the move would have been extremely difficult. At 0130 hours on 17 December, the company arrived at RJ931022, where it was met by the antitank officer of the 99th Infantry Division and the commander of the 801st Tank Destroyer Battalion. The antitank officer stated that B Company's mission was to protect the right flank of the 99th Infantry Division from armored attack. One platoon would go into an assembly area in the vicinity of RJ931022 and at dawn would take up a defensive position covering the road leading north from St. Vith. The reinforced company, minus one platoon, was to proceed to Honsfeld under the guidance of the 801st Tank Destroyer's company commander. In the Honsfeld area, the company would employ one platoon south of town at dawn, while holding the other platoon in mobile reserve within the town.

B Company, minus one platoon, moved into Honsfeld without incident. The company commander of the 801st Tank Destroyer Battalion, whose unit had been in the area for some time, ordered the commander of B Company of the 612th Tank Destroyer Battalion to bed his men for the night, and stated that at dawn he would direct the company to its position.

In addition, A Troop, 32nd Cavalry Reconnaissance Squadron, arrived in Honsfeld late in that evening. A Troop of the 32nd Cavalry Reconnaissance Squadron and remnants of the 18th Cavalry Reconnaissance Squadron were disposed along the Herresbach–Andler–Holzheim line. This position was known as Delay Position #1, and the 32nd reported to Group Headquarters (at Meyerode) that it was in this position at 1600 hours on 16 December. At 1700 hours, the remnants of the 18th Cavalry Reconnaissance Squadron (G Troop, E Troop, and F Company) moved from Holzheim–Honsfeld–Heppenbach to Wereth. Thus, the 32nd Cavalry Reconnaissance Squadron was left to hold Delay Position #1.

At 2115 hours, A Troop of the 32nd Cavalry Reconnaissance Squadron notified squadron headquarters that it had no left flak protection and that it was moving to Honsfeld. In Honsfeld, A Troop found a captain, the director of the 99th Infantry Division's rest camp, organizing the defense of the town. A few rounds of artillery were falling in the town. A Troop was to defend the town's center, while members of infantry and tank destroyer units were placed on the outskirts to defend the approaches of the town to the south and southeast. The 99th officer asked the troop commander, First Lieutenant Reppa, to provide some foot patrols to the south and southeast at first light. Reppa said that he would provide them, if orders from his squadron did not prevent.

Soldiers take a break.

At around 0500 hours on 17 December, tanks were heard generally in front by the men of the 801st Tank Destroyer, who had their guns just outside protecting the road coming in from Lanzerath. Sergeant Gallagher of the 1st RCN platoon, who was acting as outpost for 3rd Platoon, A Company, was sent out to investigate and found two American light tanks with English speaking personnel. But, still suspicious, they started to investigate further and were taken prisoner. These were elements of Skorzeny's unit, whose unit was mixed with *Kampfgruppe Peiper* (Battle Group Peiper), but the column had already reached Honsfeld.

Oberschütze Walter Wittlinger of the staff of *II./Fallschirmjäger-Regiment 9* recollects: "It still was night, 17 December, the order

'Onto the tanks—mount up!' came. I myself was sitting on a King Tiger. Now the 2nd Battalion was the point of the attack. Past Lanzerath, we turned left. We drove through the Buchholz Forest with occasional short halts. We did not dismount. Also we felt well protected. It was nicely warm on the tank, and we did not have to walk. But if we had known what was waiting for us, we would not have been so careless. For us there was no contact with the enemy. I still remember the forestry house and the sawmill near Buchholz Station very well. We drove on, still mounted on the tanks. During a slow ride as we drove into the village of Honsfeld, we saw light in the houses. In the streets jeeps and trucks were parked. In many jeeps the ignition keys were still in them, and the red lights were still burning. As we found out later, we had driven straight into a rest area of an American unit. At the time we wondered why the Americans did not stir. Probably they were surprised by the tank noise. To this day I can still see the many bundles of telephone cables. Certainly the Americans will have passed the report that German tanks have driven into Honsfeld to the rear.

"Approximately near the cemetery, we dismounted from our tanks. The tank unit drove on, apparently in the direction of Liege (?). Together with Major Taubert, First Lieutenant Gutermann and several comrades we entered a nearby farm. Day had begun. Here we found two soldiers in German Army uniforms with a radio. One soldier was sitting on a machine, like a bicycle, as it was used in earlier days, and was pedaling away to generate electricity for the radio. At the time I gave no thought about the presence of both radiomen. I can remember very well what I asked one of the signalers: what had he passed along over the radio, and he answered: 'We are jammed by Americans. He is on our frequency. We cannot get through.' I said: 'And the stand-by frequency?' 'Yes, here as well there is no connection anymore, as we are being jammed by the Americans.' Later on, and even today, I still doubt the identity of those signalers. After all, how did signalers in army uniform get here to Honsfeld? After all, our unit was the first to get into Honsfeld. Likewise, I cannot remember that army

signalers belonged to our unit. After all, we had our own
signalers. Both signalers spoke perfect German. Of course I
cannot prove that they were not Germans. *Oberleutnant* Gutermann also experienced this, and now, as I recently learned, he
has passed away.

"The orders were to move from house to house and capture the Americans present. But this order had come much
too late. It became clear that it was not very easy to execute.
The Americans put up a tough resistance. And again, there
was a sniper who fired at everything within his field of fire. It
was not possible to recover a man seriously wounded with a
headshot, as the sniper prevented this. Even when a medic
wanted to recover the wounded man, he was fired on by the
sniper as well. Because of this there were several losses. The
medics clearly were recognizable by Red Cross flags, a Red
Cross on the helmet, a Red Cross armlet, and Red Cross sheets
on the front and back. But this action did not happen every
day. Only when we had found out where the sniper stuck and
captured him, the wounded man could be recovered. We were
lucky that the SS came up with more tanks and supported our
unit in this battle. Who knows how many losses we would have
suffered otherwise. An antiaircraft tank with a four-barreled
gun (SS) shot down a fighter-bomber."

Seregeant Gallagher of the 1st RCN, 801st Tank Destroyer
Battalion, writes: "When I returned from the battalion command post around 0300 hours, I met elements of the 18th
Cavalry moving back. I was told that we should not fire on
tanks, unless we could identify them. At around 0515 hours, a
column of tanks came up the road and stopped. I and another
member of our platoon moved forward to see if it was the 18th
Cav. As we walked toward the lead tank, I was struck on my
head. My buddy could escape, but I was taken to the rear of
the column and questioned by an American speaking officer
[numerous Germans spoke English very well]. The officer told
me we were surrounded and I should surrender our troops
(this officer knew I was with the tank destroyers!). I agreed to
walk back and surrender our section. When I walked back, I

heard vehicles everywhere, so I told the German escort I was unable to find my section. We than walked back towards the tank. Then I saw the opportunity to make a break for the open field, and escaped, under heavy small arms fire. I then escaped and reached friendly lines and reported all this to the S-3 of the Engineer Battalion. By that time the Germans had already entered Honsfeld and captured nearly all."

Throughout the hours of darkness, American traffic poured through Honsfeld, most of it going to the north and northwest. These motor columns were using "cat-eye" head-lights and frequently were preceded by a soldier guiding the vehicles with a flashlight. It was a very dark night. At about 0500 on 17 December, Sergeant Creel, commander of an armored car (A Troop of 32nd Cavalry Group) that had been positioned to defend the center of the town from attack from the southeast saw a figure with a flashlight guiding a tank by Creel's vehicle. As the tank came abreast of the armored car, Creel saw a large swastika on the side of the tank; at that same moment, heavy small-arms fire began a hundred yards down the road from the car.

In the furor that followed, Creel observed that enemy tanks were firing into the building that had housed the com-mand post of the elements defending the town, and that the infantry and tank destroyer troops stationed at the southeast-ern approach to the town came streaming back along the road in disorder. Creel's car had a trailer attached to its rear. This prevented his car from firing at the enemy. The three compa-nies of troops in that area were evacuated, and the men hur-ried to join 2nd Lt. John V. Harmon's platoon which was in position in the western sector of the town. By the time the men had reached there via the backyards and alleys, the impetus of the enemy attack had carried the enemy armor around his position, and Harmon directed the men to withdraw. He was convinced the town had been overrun with enemy armor. Split into two groups, Sgt. John S. Catanese and Lieutenant Har-mon led eighteen- and fourteen-man groups, respectively, out of Honsfeld. Moving westward and cross-country, these rem-nants of A Troop rejoined the group at Mirfeld.

Obersturmführer Werner Sternebeck of the *1st SS-Panzer-Division "Leibstandarte"* recalls: "At approximately 0430 hours, we reached Honsfeld. In town, standing on the right side of the road in our direction, was an armored column (tanks, half-tracks, jeeps)—a reconnaissance unit. Since I thought it was a unit from 'Einsatzgruppe Greif,' I stopped next to the column to make contact. I dismounted from my panzer and climbed onto the other and looked for the 'Z' designation on the turret. Unfortunately, my search was in vain; I was standing next to the enemy—who dozed. My next reaction was to climb back into my panzer, beat a quick retreat to the northwestern exit from the town and report the presence of the enemy to the panzer battalion."

Karl Wortmann of the *10./(Fla) Panzer-Regiment 1, 1st SS-Panzer-Division* remembers: "I was in the Ardennes offensive from the first day to the last, and I was a tank commander and commander of a half-platoon in a newly raised armored anti-aircraft company. We partially had 3.7cm antiaircraft guns on *Panzer IV* chassis (the so-called *Möbelwagen*—'moving van'—because of the size) as well as 2cm flak guns (the so-called *Wirbelwind*—'whirlwind'—because of the firepower), partially mounted on the *Panzer IV's*. The latter was a so-called quick-firing weapon. Our first tank platoon was a mixed one; we had four tanks, two *Möbelwagens*, and two *Wirbelwinds*. At the start of the Ardennes offensive, which really kicked off on 17 December 1944, we drove well at the front of the column. We had been divided into marching columns by platoons. On the stretch from Lanzerath to Buchholz Station, we suffered fierce enemy fire for a brief moment. The enemy had withdrawn to Buchholz Station.

"Our column split up before the village of Honsfeld. Part of the main street through the village was very narrow and had a lot of curves. In it both our tanks and a Möbelwagen were knocked out at close range from the entrance of a house. The third and fourth tanks were Wirbelwinds. I controlled the third tank. I noticed the flame from the barrel of the enemy anti-tank gun. With a few bursts of fire, I knocked out the antitank gun. The two *Möbelwagens*, which had been hit, were no longer capable of continuing. Some of the crews were severely wounded. In the next house the Yanks were firing from the higher floors into the armored personnel carriers that followed us and which had open tops. The fight was short but fierce. My tank continued to drive to the exit of the village and remained standing there. I went back to our two knocked-out tanks to find out what happened. Both tanks and crews were total write-offs.

"I returned again to our *Wirbelwinds*. My comrades told me that by now they were standing opposite the cemetery, and that they had seen something move behind the tombstones. It was a combat unit of 'Skorzeny,' a group of German troops, which operated in American uniform. That was the German detachment 'Greif,' which had been trained for several months for this operation and which were to render us many good services later. The fighter-bomber attack at Buchholz Station lasted only a short while and was driven off by our four anti-aircraft tanks which at that time were still operational. The kills of the two *Möbelwagens* followed later directly in the village of Honsfeld. From Honsfeld Cemetery, both antiaircraft tanks continued toward Büllingen, and we took the guys from Operation Greif with us on our tanks."

Rudi Frühbeisser of *Fallschirmjäger-Regiment 9* writes: "Now that Honsfeld lies in front of us in the beginning dawn, our tank stops. At a wink of our commander, the entire company dismounts. Immediately we penetrate into the houses on our right and left. Here it is swarming with Yanks. Without the company knowing, we had driven straight into the rest camp of the U.S. 99th Infantry Division and the U.S. 394th Infantry Regiment. The Yankees are disarmed straight away and their weapons rendered unusable. Then they're driven onto the street. Well, that is good booty for our commander. He is still waiting for the regimental commander, who is supposed to have been mounted up with the commander of the second battalion. Our commander finds *Major* Taubert, the commander of the 2nd Battalion, but our regimental commander is not with him. The regimental commander is supposed to have been picked up and sitting on the last tank. Until the regimental commander arrives, *Freiherr* von Schenk takes over the command of the regiment. Suddenly, when we want to mount up again, the fireworks start. From nearly all windows in the vicinity, a hail of fire rains down on the paratroopers that are standing around. We open fire straightaway. American mortars are firing as well, and they're not firing badly. Already the first groups are bounding back towards the village. Our tank turns his 88mm gun and fires on a machine gun. Direct hit! By now the first houses are being retaken and the Yanks are thrown out. Many Yanks fall in the fire of machine guns and machine pistols. We also suffer our first losses. *Oberschütze* Munz of the regimental staff gets a belly shot that is hopeless. Of the 1st Company, *Gefreiter* Hauprich falls, and *Gefreiter* Biehl gets a grazing shot to the head. *Oberschütze* Otto Schipotini was also hit. *Oberleutnant* Later is hit by shrapnel in the leg. *Gefreiter* Schilling and *Gefreiter* Pfeifer, who are storming forward with him, are also hit."

Jim Foley, H Company 394th Infantry Regiment, 99th Infantry Division, describes the situation in Honsfeld in a letter to company-mate Rex Whitehead (who left Honsfeld on the afternoon of 16 December): "About 10 P.M., stuff started flying into the town. We didn't think much of it. After all, they told us, it was just a little heavy patrol action. (What a patrol!) Then a shell blew hell out of the improvised shower across the street. We were getting pretty worried, but I wasn't going to get out of that sleeping bag until they blew me out. About 2 A.M., we heard vehicles in the street. What worried us was that they were going the wrong way. They were our Recon cars going back to division headquarters. Still, we stayed in the sack until after 5 A.M., when we heard some heavy vehicles in the street. We didn't have any tanks in the area, so I decided to take a look. Before I had a chance, I heard a shot outside, and Wooten from G Company ran into the room. All he had on were his long johns, and he looked funny as hell. He said, 'One of those silly damn guards of ours took a shot at me when I stepped out to take a piss!' It was all very funny at the time, but what we didn't know was that the 'guard' happened to be a Jerry. I piled back into the sack until 6:30 A.M. when I hear Kraut voices in the street. It was confusing to say the least, so I hopped up to take a look. I stuck my head outside to see a few of our recon car's burning across the street and three Kraut tanks very much intact! Then some bastard opened up on me with a burp gun, and I got my ass back inside quick. We barricaded the door and decided to make a break out the back window. We changed our mind when we saw the fields crawling with Jerry infantry. We were stuck but good. So we sat on the floor, me with my trusty .45 which couldn't hit a B-29 at ten paces, and waited. The next thing we heard was that the Staff Sergeant from E Company was going to surrender the whole rest camp. After a few minutes of horrible confusion, we were all lined up outside with a bunch of stupid Supermen screaming like crazy at us. I hated to give up like that but I guess it was the best thing to do. We didn't have so much as a BAR in the whole place. If we had started shooting, we would have been slaughtered like a bunch of cattle."

Standartenführer Joachim Peiper, commander of *Kampfgruppe Peiper*, recollects: "The entrance of the village was guarded by antitank guns. In position but unarmed! The whole place was crammed with armored vehicles, obviously belonging to a reconnaissance battalion, but again deserted. We fire at everything while sweeping through the little town, in order to cause panic and to secure the rear exit. And panic did arise. It was a disturbed group. Half clad soldiers either surrendered or tried to escape. No resistance to speak of. I ordered the commanding officer of the parachute battalion that accompanied me to stay in Honsfeld, mop up the place and to await further orders from his regiment. In all, our booty consisted of fifty reconnaissance vehicles, including half-tracks; about thirty two-and-a-half-ton trucks; and fifteen or sixteen antitank guns. My combat group then proceeded to Büllingen, receiving some small-arms fire, but this didn't make us unhappy, because although there was a slight delay, it allowed rear vehicles to close up."

Modern view of a house in Honsfeld. J. WIJERS

Oberschütze Walter Wittlinger of the *II./Fallschirmjäger-Regiment 9*, writes: "After the end of the battle in Honsfeld, both sides had taken losses. The American prisoners were brought to the hall in the inn Eifeler Hof. There they were guarded until they could be transported to the rear. Even before the end of the battle, I was in the hall of the inn. Here everything had been prepared for Christmas. One decorated Christmas tree stood in the hall. I still remember well that I drank a beer here. In the hall, as I remember it, there were over 100 prisoners. Among them there was a captain. This I know, as I was detailed to guard them while my comrades searched for, and found, something edible.

"While I was guarding the prisoners, three soldiers, partially dressed in American uniform, came up and asked me to collect various bits of American equipment from the prisoners for them. At that time, the entrance to the hall was separated from the street by an entrance room. I told them, 'Anyone can come and demand this!' Now one of the three said, 'According to *Führer* orders, anyone who objects to us can be shot on the spot without trial!' Now I demanded their papers. Silently they showed their Army pay books (identification cards). I had to conclude that they were an SS officer and two SS NCOs. After seeing this information, I told them, 'Get the kit

German paratroopers collect American uniform parts in Honsfeld. On the street are dead American soldiers, most likely from the tank destroyer unit defending the center of town. U.S. ARMY

yourselves!' Even today I wonder at my courage in saying something like that to an SS officer. No one would have made a fuss if they had shot me on the spot. I can only assume that they wanted to make as little fuss as possible. I went with them into the hall and saw them take rubber overshoes and steel helmets from the prisoners. Apart from this activity, I did not see anything illegal. After the three had got their equipment, they got in a jeep and drove off. I don't know where. I have to mention here that during this action nothing that was against the Geneva convention happened. For our side I know that, apart from weapons, no personal possessions were taken and no maltreatment occurred. A big booty was captured, but everything had to go to the rear."

CHAPTER 4

Operations of the 16th Infantry Regiment

The U.S. 1st Infantry Division's 16th Infantry Regiment (less the 2nd Battalion) was relieved by the 28th Infantry Division on 11 December 1944 and went into rest area near Verviers, where the 2nd Battalion was loaned on 13 December to the 26th Infantry Regiment, 1st Infantry Division. Under the control of VII Corps, these units engaged in training and recreational activities until 16 December. The 1st and 3rd Battalions of the 16th Infantry Regiment closed in their new area at 0030 hours on 18 December, 1944. Between 0130 hours and 0450 hours, the 30th Infantry Division passed through the 16th Infantry's positions to a new area.

At 0840 hours on 18 December, a report from the 16th Infantry Regiment on its disposition of forces indicated that the 1st and 3rd Battalions were in the line: the 3rd Battalion coming into the area along the stream north of Weywertz and the 1st Battalion extending around Busbach. One company was left in Robertville to cover the bridge over its lake at that point. Patrols from the 16th Infantry Regiment were able to report that the following towns were clear of the enemy at 1515 hours: Weywertz, Bütgenbach, Waimes, Road, Champagne, Bruyères, Walk, Longfaye, and Xhoffraix. One platoon of the Belgian 5th Füsilier Battalion was in Xhoffraix and two sections of this unit were in Longfaye. By 1605 hours, a patrol from the 16th Infantry Regiment reported the town of Chôdes was clear from enemy troops.

During the afternoon of 18 December, Task Force Davisson—consisting of Headquarters, Medical Detachment,

Modern views of Robertville in the direction of Bütgenbach
(south) from where American troops expected the German
advance. J. WIJERS

and the Reconnaissance Company of the 634th Tank
Destroyer Battalion (Self Propelled), one company of light
tanks of the 745th Tank Battalion and one platoon of the 1st
Reconnaissance Troop, 1st Infantry Division—was organized
and ordered to secure the town of Waimes. B Company, 1st
Engineer Combat Battalion of the 1st Infantry Division, and

one platoon of the 703rd Tank Destroyer Battalion were later put in support of this group. By 1700 hours, the task force had entered Waimes and had started the evacuation of the 47th Evacuation Hospital and D Company 99th Medical Battalion (Collecting Company) of the 99th Infantry Division. Attempts by small forces of German paratroopers of the *3rd Fallschirmjäger-Division* and elements of *Kampfgruppe Peiper* of the *1st SS-Panzer-Division* to enter the town during the night were unsuccessful.

Private First Class "Smilin' Al" Alvarez of C Company, 16th Infantry Regiment, Task Force Davisson, remembers: "'Recon, you find 'em; engineers, you fix 'em; tanks, you fight 'em; and TD's, you finish 'em!' With these emphatic, but crystal-clear adjurations, Lt. Col. Henry L. Davisson set the tempo for his task force subordinate commanders. In response to the German tank penetration, hastily thrown together units from the vaunted 1st Infantry Division would acquire its title 'from the aggressive commander of the 634th Tank Destroyer Battalion.' Task Force Davisson was thus quickly formed as a lightly armored, tank-killing reaction force! Major Olson, the Task Force Davisson's S-3, designated the line of march and handed out strip-maps for a southward reconnaissance.

"Our armored convoy consisted of the 1st Recon Troops heading out with puny 37mm armed M8 Greyhound armored cars. Intermingled came the 1st Combat Engineer Battalion's A Company riding its soft-skinned vehicles. Now came D Company of the 745th Tank Battalion with its measly Whippert tanks armed with 37mm guns (M5 Stuart), but backed up by its 75mm assault gun platoon. Spread out and looking for targets came C Company of the 634th Tank Destroyer Battalion (M10) with their 90mm guns, claiming the ability to compete with German armor. All ably supported by 'the king of the battlefield,' our four-man 'F.O. Charlie' Arty Observation party (with the common capability to call down division artillery and corps artillery—'barrages or serenades').

"Our battery veterans of the 'Lucky 7th' Artillery Battalion, who had fought German armor in Tunisia, Algeria, the beach

Al Alvarez.

of Sicily, and in the fields of Normandy, spoke out in warning to our little observer party: 'Be ready. . . . The huge Panther outguns this task force and King Tiger monsters are reported coming your way. . . . Remember, your tank-destroying force needs to equal or outgun those battle-tested German behemoths and also mount sufficient armor to protect themselves from the superior German antitank weapon. In other words, you better be 'killer tanks' rather than 'tank killers.' If not, you will have to stop 'em with indirect 105mm or 155mm arty concentrations.'

"Despite these knowledgeable words, we heard only the spurrings of Colonel Davisson. Quickly, the task force saddled up and cautiously commenced traveling south through snowy

Modern views of Waimes, showing the roads leading to the south and east out of the town. This is where Task Force Davisson took up its position. HANS WIJERS

Belgium. The lengthy convoy slid out of Sourbrodt and Robertville and clanked into Walk and Waimes, small villages recently vacated by U.S. medical units."

Later that evening, Task Force Davisson reported that they had established six roadblocks on the east, south, and west of Waimes. The 703rd Tank Destroyer Battalion (M36s) was

Modern view of the school at Waimes, which was packed with army vehicles of the field hospital during the battle. HANS WIJERS

Joe Rowley of the I&R Platoon of the 16th Infantry Regiment
talks to civilians in Waimes. The soldier with the helmet is
Wheeler, and on the right edge is Bill Wheatly. After the war,
Rowley visited the author and Karl-Heinz Heck in Bütgenbach.
They tracked down the young man in the picture, Leon Rosen,
who remembered every detail of the photo, including the fact
that this is winter 1944, despite the fairly lightweight clothing,
which was all they had. JOE ROWLEY

attached to the U.S. 1st Infantry Division as of 1300 hours, 17
December.

Charles E. Schaffer of B Company, 1st Engineer Combat
Battalion, recalls: "That afternoon, we (B Company) were sent
to defend Waimes and to rescue an evacuation hospital in the
vicinity. Later some tank destroyers, a light tank company and

part of the First Reconnaissance Troop joined the company. Roadblocks were established and defensive positions were set up. During the night, several small enemy units attempted to enter the town but were quickly repulsed."

Lieutenant Colonel Robert F. Evans, G-2 of the 703rd Tank Destroyer Battalion, writes: "The 1st Infantry Division, in addition to its own 57mm guns, had its normal tank destroyer battalion, the 634th (self-propelled 3-inch), attached and integrated, with tank destroyer platoons attached to infantry battalions. The mission of the 703rd Tank Destroyer Battalion was, operating under battalion control, to initiate immediate reconnaissance of routes and gun position areas on the division left flank and be prepared to repel any armored thrusts that might get through friendly troops on our left. This mission was given because our left flank was not yet fully stabilized, and up to that time, enemy pressure was strongest from that direction.

"In the meantime, shortly after noon, a task force was hastily organized from whatever units were available at the moment to proceed to Waimes and protect the evacuation of a field hospital located there. The second platoon of A Company joined this task force and moved out at 1400 hours. The task force was under command of Lieutenant Colonel Davisson of the 634th Tank Destroyer Battalion. It was found at Waimes that the hospital had already been evacuated, and the task force remained in that area to secure the town."

CHAPTER 5

The *3rd Fallschirmjäger-Division* Attacks

Hauptfeldwebel Fritz Roppelt, forward observer in the 12th Company of *Fallschirmjäger-Regiment 9, 3rd Fallschirmjäger-Division*, remembers: "In the early morning of 18 December, we received the order that we had to move on in the direction of Thirimont. We had loaded our 8cm mortars, grenades, and U.S. supplies (captured during the fighting for Hill 587 between Hergersberg and Berterath) on U.S. carts. The paratrooper officer in charge of the *3rd Fallschirmjäger-Division* had returned a message by radio that we should use the twilight in the evening. The fully motorized 12cm mortars were already in Thirimont, which could allow us some time. In the dark we arrived at Thirimont. The same night, we had to move out to Ondenval, exactly on the borderline area between *Fallschirmjäger-Regiment 5* and *Fallschirmjäger-Regiment 9*.

"When we arrived in Ondenval, we hardly had a choice where to build our mortar position because the battalions of the regiment, which was already there before us, had occupied the best coverage options. The paratroopers felt more safe if the mortar position was farther away from them. So we found, farther to the rear, a perfect position between the church and the priest house. It was protected from the back and the sides against *Jabo* [fighter-bomber] attacks and had a place for our mortars, while at the same time giving good protection for the troops at the front line.

"Like all mortar units from 8cm, we were placed under direct command of the division. Often, it did not work with the food. As a platoon commander, I was the oldest at the age of

Fritz Roppelt.

just twenty-one. The young paratroopers of seventeen, eighteen, nineteen years had the biggest hunger. Preserves and wine shouldn't have been stolen from the former reverend. I can only apologize for my soldiers. On the other hand, I was almost constantly on the road, on forward observation posts, and there was nothing to stop the hunger of young soldiers."

The situation report of Army Group B for 19 December 1944 contains the following information about the situation in the sector of the *3rd Fallschirmjäger-Division*: "*3rd Fallschirmjäger-Division* is attacking toward Weywertz from the line Morsheck–Möderscheid." The daily report of *OB West* for 19 December states: "*3rd Fallschirmjäger-Division* with two regimental groups north of Schoppen. One regimental group gained ground just to the south of Roymonville [Faymonville]."

Between 19 December and Christmas Day, elements of the German *12th SS-Panzer-Division "Hitlerjugend"* and supporting units, such as *Sturmpanzer-Abteilung 217*, tried again and again

Modern view of the priest house (left) and church (right) in Ondenval. HANS WIJERS

Modern view from the church. HANS WIJERS

to take Bütgenbach. During this heavy fighting, elements of the *3rd Fallschirmjäger-Division* had dug in on the left side of the *12th SS-Panzer-Division* roughly south of the road between Bütgenbach and Malmédy.

Rudi Frühbeisser of *Fallschirmjäger-Regiment 9* wrote a dayby-day account of the actions with his unit: "19 December—at 0800 hours, the 1st Battalion receives orders that we have to

Guy Sajec of the 16th Infantry Regiment. MRS. SAJEC

march immediately to Hepscheid. The 2nd Battalion stays in the Morsheck area in its positions, and the 3rd Battalion is kept in reserve. At the moment, the 1st Battalion is moving out of its positions; it is receiving heavy enemy artillery fire. Again we have to run for our lives.

"At 0900 hours, we receive orders through a runner from regimental headquarters that the battalion must return to its former positions at the Domaine Bütgenbach, which is now 1,900 meters behind us, to attack the U.S. positions. We should attack at 1300 hours!

"Halfway down the road another runner brings a new order: 'The 1st Battalion is to march for the Schoppen area immediately in order to beat off an expected attack with tanks.' So about-face again!"

Task Force Davisson, which had evacuated American units from Waimes on 18 December, became apprehensive as to its own position the following morning. At 1100 hours on 19 December, the 1st Infantry Division was told that the enemy was building up his force outside the town. Earlier, at 1000 hours, contact had been made with two armored cars and several German soldiers at location 852026 while enemy tanks were reported at the hill outside the town, and a Mark IV or V (Panther) was said to be coming into the town itself. The Task Force indicated that it was not strong enough to deal with a strong infantry attack or a small tank attack. The 16th Infantry Regiment replied that the task force should sit tight since aid was on the way from the 2nd Battalion.

By 1345 hours, the 2nd Battalion had moved up its anti-tank guns and its M10 tank destroyers. E Company was preparing to move within fifteen minutes, and it was to be followed by the 3rd Battalion within an hour. By 1725 hours, the 3rd Battalion was engaging the enemy to the east of Waimes, while G Company was fighting in the western and E Company in the eastern portion of town. The 2nd Battalion took over the responsibility for the defense of the town that evening.

CHAPTER 6

The German Attack on Belair

Units of the 16th Infantry Regiment, 1st Infantry Division, carried on small actions at Belair during the evening of 19 December 1944. I Company of the 3rd Battalion established its flank at that town, while F and K Companies built up their positions south of the road from Waimes to Bütgenbach.

The *3rd Fallschirmjäger-Division* was attacking in the sector Weywertz–Waimes. Elements of *Fallschirmjäger-Regiment 9* under the command of *Oberst i.G.* von Hoffmann coming from the area Morsheck–Schoppen moved in the direction of Faymonville.

Oberschütze Rudi Frühbeisser of *Fallschirmjäger-Regiment 9* recollects: "By 1800 hours on 19 December, the battalion arrives in Schoppen, which is taken without a fight. All are so tired that they fall over, as today we covered a large number of miles because of the continual turnabouts. Even though we now have several jeeps which carry the greater part of the heavy munitions chests, the personal equipment of the men remains heavy. Immediately we begin with the erection of provisional positions."

Oberschütze Günther Meyer of the 3rd Company, 1st Battalion, *Fallschirmjäger-Regiment 9*, writes: "On the evening of 19 December, we had dug ourselves in at the outskirts of Schoppen. Outposts were set up, and so, though being cold and wet, we could get a few hours of sleep. Suddenly, our rest was disturbed by an incoming order from the 1st Battalion: The next morning at 0545 hours, the 1st Battalion was ordered to march in the direction of Faymonville, and secure the town to the west (Steinbach in the direction towards Waimes) and to the north (Belair) against enemy tank attack."

Oberst i.G. von Hoffmann.

The war diary of the 16th Infantry Regiment contains the following entry for 19 December at 2330 hours: "Situation report from Faymonville. About fifty enemy soldiers are in the outskirts of the town. They rushed in the first houses at Belair in groups of eight to ten. I Company's right flank is the first house at Belair. We have been killing a lot of enemy up there. They moved in, since we came up. We have people in that house and F and K Companies are tied in at the junction at 858037. K Company is just north of the road over to the next junction at 867. I Company is in the coordinate 879. F Company's right flank is 852033; they have roadblocks there. E Company is on the flank of a stream at 850026 and comes across the main road out, right flank at 849027. Have contact with C Company, 120th Infantry Regiment (30th Infantry Division) and have joint outposts."

Frühbeisser again: "20 December 1944—total losses: 85 men (8 killed, 73 wounded, 2 missing, and 2 prisoners). At

Günther Meyer.

0545 hours, a renewed order: 'The 1st Battalion is to march to Faymonville straightaway, in order to defend the village against enemy tank attacks from the north and west!'

"After a long, difficult march, we arrive in Faymonville at 0815 hours. Here the Yankees also have abandoned everything in a hurry. If things continue this way, soon every soldier in our unit can drive his own vehicle.

"Here a nice surprise is waiting for the 1st Battalion. Our battalion commander here learns that he and his battalion are under the command of a young captain of *Fallschirmjäger-Regiment 5*. Immediately orders come to attack the village of Belair, which lies 800 meters to the north of the road, which comes from Waimes and leads to Bütgenbach. The village itself consists of six houses and a chapel. But orders are orders, even though they're idiotic."

Günther Meyer continues his story: "When we—without enemy resistance—entered Faymonville, the enemy left the town and abandoned their vehicles. Their quarters were still full with all kind of stuff; food and cigarettes everywhere.

"Suddenly, we got the order to attack Belair. The *Fallschirm-jäger* units were at the front line as normal infantry, without any support of heavy weapons (no tanks or artillery). The only support we got was from six mortars. We also didn't have any winter clothing or camouflaged uniforms. This attack was against all we had learned, and I could only guess that we would be offered for 'higher meanings'! And what were we going to attack? We didn't see any *Amis*!

"Attack at 1500 hours! The 3rd Company was attacking from a house situated left next to the street Faymonville, north to Fosse de Loup (in the direction of Belair), about 500 to 600 meters from the center of the town, into the street that bends to the right, to the street that goes to the north into a secondary road that ends after 250 meters. The weather was mixed—that means snow, ice, but also mud. Woods and fields full of melting snow made it muddier and quite difficult to move forward. Then the temperature went down again (freezing)."

Frühbeisser picks up his account: "It is an unusual task as we are lying here alone in a wide open terrain. Furthermore, we don't have any heavy weapons to support us. The forward observer can't make any contact with our own artillery for a change.

"When we're approaching, we're shelled nicely by the Yanks. Our 'old man' has grave doubts, as the Yanks are far ahead of us in their combat preparations. Because an attack without artillery preparation is against all the basic rules of tactics and only is pure slaughter. Despite this the attack is fixed for 1500 hours by the young captain. Six mortars of *Fallschirm-jäger-Regiment 8* are to support us. But where are they to fire anyway, as we haven't discovered any American positions.

"When our commander inspects the assembly areas, the Americans shell it with a murderous mortars fire. To get through at this point will be hectic.

"Then the order to attack comes. When the battalion wants to move out of the assembly area the fireworks begin! There

Modern view of the road leading into Schoppen. HANS WIJERS

must be a forward observer around somewhere in the area who is directing the fire so well, or it could not fall so well aimed. It is impossible to even gain a few meters. Wounded are crying out everywhere. Our commander does not follow the order to leave the 1st Battalion behind in the little wood, if one can talk of a little wood here anyway. The wood had been completely plowed under and partially begins to burn, as the Yanks are again firing phosphorus shells. Then the rounds hiss through the air so that one imagines one's head is being taken off. Slowly, taking our dead and wounded with us, the battalion withdraws towards Faymonville. Our gracious captain finally gives us permission to withdraw. The withdrawing troops continuously are harassed by American artillery and mortar fire. Many wounded cannot be recovered anymore, for as soon as the ambulances tried to advance, a blocking barrage blocked their way."

Back to Günther Meyer: "On this road I was sent with my group of fourteen *Fallschirmjäger* (we had two MG42 machine guns with us) by *Hauptmann* Woitschek (company commander, 3rd Company, 1st Battalion, *Fallschirmjäger-Regiment 9*). He was standing along the road, waving with his hand, holding a P38

Oberleutnant Udo Balfanz, commander of
the 3rd Battalion of *Fallschirmjäger-
Regiment 5*. He was promoted to *Major* on
1 January 1945.

pistol, and telling us in which direction we should go, then he
was gone. At the entrance of the road, we saw a couple of dead
American soldiers. It looked like we were the only attacking
force in the whole area!

"Shortly before we reached the small forest, we entered a
road with pine trees left and right as high as six meters. The
enemy artillery and mortar fire was getting stronger and
stronger, and within an hour it was unbearable! Suddenly, I
was alone with my machine gunner, *Oberschütze* Steinebrunner.
Where were the other twelve men of my group? There was no
cover, just lie flat on the ground hoping you wouldn't get hit
by shrapnel or even a direct hit.

Oberstleutnant Gundolf *Freiherr* Schenk zu
Schweinsberg, commander of the 1st
Battalion, *Fallschirmjäger-Regiment 9.*

"Then something unbelievable happened. In front of us
on the road stood a *Fallschirmjäger*. At that moment a grenade
hit the ground next to him. Because of the pressure of the
explosion, he was thrown through the air, four or five meters
high. The big trees were waving from left to right due to the
pressure, and then he came down on his feet on the muddy
ground next to the street, stood for a few seconds, cleaned his
jacket, put his helmet on, that lay next to him, and moved on!
He didn't have a scratch! Shortly after that, another hit in
front of us. A *Fallschirmjäger* from my company, who I knew
personally very well, came running down the street and was hit
by shrapnel. He got hit badly on his right hip and didn't look

too well at the time. He tried to reach the other side of the road, and I lost track of him. Did he manage to get back to Faymonville? I don't know, never saw him again.

"The artillery fire got more and more intense, and hit the small forest were we thought we were safe—at that moment I wouldn't give a penny for my life. As we looked southwest, we saw a quarry. There we saw about ten to fifteen *Fallschirmjäger* trying to dig a hole with their hands. But digging a hole in these stone parts didn't work, and the artillery found them as well. Also these *Fallschirmjäger* comrades wouldn't survive the heavy artillery fire if they didn't find cover very soon.

"I had the feeling that no one would come out of this small forest alive. The noise of battle, the artillery fire, it was all so loud, you didn't hear the screaming of the wounded. I couldn't think of how medics would go in there and try to rescue the wounded *Fallschirmjäger*. Did we even have some with us up here? I hadn't seen one!

"The light-bright edge of the forest, approximately 150 meters away, was in view. The edge of the forest was not a 'safe harbor' for either of us, because probably somewhere in the field in front of us would be the main line of resistance, covered with entrenched enemy infantry. No enemy to be seen, also the enemy rifle and machine gun fire was neither visible nor audible. The edge of forest was along the road Bütgenbach–Oberweywertz–Belair–Waimes. The *Ami* then fired phosphorus shells. Shrapnel projectiles from large-caliber artillery, which exploded over us in the trunks and branches of the trees that rained down on us was hell! The fight offered no prospects with an invisible opponent! We fought four or five days against an enemy who didn't allow any ground gains of the German aggressors!

"I was 150 meters from the edge of forest, along the road from Belair. Steinebrunner was badly wounded by a shrapnel fragment which had split his lower jaw. In order to keep his jaw intact, he had to press it slightly with both blood-smeared hands to his head! I was wounded at the same time with three shrapnel fragments in my left thigh. Although I was in pain, I

Modern view of the road to Belair. The little forest is at right.

Modern view from the forest to the Waimes–Bütgenbach road.

HANS WIJERS

assumed that no bones, at least not my knees or legs, were badly hit.

"I lifted the relatively large Steinebrunner under his right shoulder, and thus we tried to escape 'to the rear' from the forest. We dragged ourselves along the quarry to the road, leading to Faymonville. The road's deep tank-tracks in the snow, protected us against impacts, and we reached Faymonville before the darkness, probably as some other wounded did."

Frühbeisser again: "Then the grenades ricochet through the air with a hissing sound, which one thinks his head gets blow away! Slowly, carrying the dead and wounded with us, the battalion retreats on the outskirts from Faymonville. The 'gracious' Captain granted the permission that we could withdraw.

"Constantly, the retreating troops were bombarded by American grenade and mortar fire. Many wounded were not recovered. Because as soon as medics were trying to recover them, a rain of all calibers of American artillery were blocking their way.

Günther Meyer continues his story: "After asking directions, we both reached the barn, 3rd Company headquarters. I believe it was at the northern part of Faymonville, less than ten meters away from our own straw camp. It was ice cold in the barn and without light. In part of the barn, *Hauptmann* Woitscheck sat in a very warm, lighted area. Woitscheck did not consider it necessary for us, the wounded of his company, to come to his room. For Steinebrunner it was a painful night; there was no medic aid, and the prospect of getting to the aid station was not a given!

"The Americans had entrenched themselves heavily in front of Belair. I have seen that before me and beside me, human body parts were swirled high in the air, during the heavy artillery barrage from the Americans. As if by a miracle, I walked away with 'only' three pieces of shrapnel. Our attack was not repeated on this day."

Oberschütze Frühbeisser resumes his narrative: "21 December 1944—total losses: 21 men (3 killed, 17 wounded, 1 missing). The 1st Company, which has shrunk to a small band, can take cover in a single cellar of a house. In the railway

Modern view of the woods near Waimes, where the paratroopers prepared to attack the surrounding towns. HANS WIJERS

Three grave sites are still visible in the woods. HANS WIJERS

embankment our wonderful staff doctor, Dr. Walter Kahle, has established his dressing station in a mining corridor. We old ones are proud of this doctor, as he always was up front without the least reticence. Often our 'old man' had to threaten the dear staff doctor with his index finger! Because our dear staff doctor would have preferred to lead a platoon or any other unit. But he has put his qualities as a doctor at the unit's disposal. Many soldiers, who were treated by the doctor, afterwards were of the opinion that he was no butcher and has a good, quieting word for everybody. We old paratroopers only grin when we see our 'carbolic uncle,' as all of us in Normandy have experienced what it's like when scalpels cut into our own flesh.

"The positions in the battalion area are so that we have the villages of Waimes, Thioux, Ruthier, Belair, Wedden and Oberweywertz in front of us. In a map study at the company commander's, we establish that we're only 3800 meters from the Elsenborn training area. Relief out of our positions can only take place at night. Here also since a few days an American spotter plane is up again and observes and registers every little movement with a bombardment by mortars. With the partially German binoculars, which we captured in Honsfeld, we spot a single heavy mortar near a house about 700 meters distance. We also can spot that from time to time a Yank comes out of the house door and fires ten rounds from the mortar! Though the impacts are in our vicinity they cause no damage. He also is firing at our heights with a jeep-mounted machine gun. Then he disappears again. Then some of the old ones have decided to get the mortar and the machine gun. On a sketch block the route that we can follow with our binoculars is sketched exactly. Well, we'll have some fun and spoil the cellar for the Yanks. These friends are sitting in their warm cellar and we're freezing in the positions.

"At the joining of the sector of the 2nd Company, a ditch is found, which ends a hundred meters in front of the house on the road. The road also to be followed in the withdrawal due to the tracks in the snow. At darkness some comrades get on with it. Among them there is an *Oberschütze* of the engineer company who has had various ideas for the fireworks. Six men are sneaking through the starry bright, cold night. On the lighting of the watches it shows that it is two o'clock. Then the ditch, which has to be a brook further up, ends with a pipe on the road. Here we jump across the road. Two men, one on each side, remain at the pipe, to cover the withdrawal. After a while the four remaining paratroopers arrive at the house. Carefully they crawl around the house, looking for trip wires and other alarms. At the back there is a jeep with trailer. The troopers hear the Americans talk through the cellar windows. Carefully one takes an American mine and hangs it from the barrel of the mortar. Quickly a fuse is attached.

"The jeep with the trailer and the jeep by the house also are prepared. On a hissing sound the fuses are ignited with a lighter. They withdraw on the double. When the sentries by the pipe have been reached, all remain standing for a short while. All blows up with a loud explosion. Shortly afterwards the house is burning as well. Quickly they crawl back. The men of the 2nd Company are waiting and should not get nervous. The agreed password had been 'fireworks.'

"Soon all have arrived at the 2nd Company in a sweat. The house by the road is burning brightly and is illuminating far and wide. After a while, a barrage falls near the house. Presumably, this was called up by the Yanks in the house after the blast. When nothing moved after that they had the rest of the day to think about what happened. By day one can see with binoculars that black smoke is coming from the cellar windows. The roof had gone and one could see through the rear wall. The load of the jeep and the trailer must have compacted the house.

"Our company commander then made us snails and forbade these extras. In the 13th Company, shrapnel through the heart kills Alfred Beck. Silvester Windermann is coming with a report from the regimental staff. In Schoppen, heavy artillery fire is falling on the southern village road, in which a splinter in the rear of the head hits Windermann; he is buried in the grounds of Nr. 17. After the battle, squad leader Banse of the 2nd Company is missing. In the 4th Company, platoon commander *Leutnant* Wilfried Frey has made himself comfortable in a house. During a shelling of the village, several shells hit the house. Frey is buried while lying in bed and is recovered with severe internal head wounds. The losses from shrapnel are increasing."

The war diary of the 16th Infantry Regiment records the following for 20 December: "At 1235 hours, the 16th Infantry Regiment told the division that their 3rd Battalion had everything under control, and they were not worried about the report that the enemy was working up the railroad; C Company was staying where they were, and A Company was taking K Company's place." The next entry, at 2100 hours, reads: "The 634th Tank Destroyer Battalion (self-propelled) was told that the division was pulling Task Force Davisson out of Waimes tomorrow morning. The tank destroyer battalion was told that the division wanted the task force to assemble north of Weywertz on the north side of the stream."

CHAPTER 7

Resistance by Elements of *Fallschirmjäger-Regiment 9* in Faymonville

Beginning Wednesday, 20 December 1944, Faymonville was the object of continuous American artillery barrages. The impacts grew more and more intense and continued without a break day and night. Faymonville was a direct frontal area, as the Americans had taken positions in Waimes.

On 21 December, action continued north of Faymonville. Again and again, the Americans tried to take Faymonville from the direction of Gueuzaine via Belair and Ruthier.

Oberschütze Günther Meyer of the 3rd Company, 1st Battalion, *Fallschirmjäger-Regiment 9* remembers: "On 21 December 1944, many of our wounded soldiers were transported back behind our own lines from Faymonville. In Montenau, the Monastery, St. Raphael, was the main aid post for the wounded that needed to be operated. My operation, without anesthesia, didn't bring any improvement; they couldn't remove the grenade fragment. I ended up only with a bandage. The whole monastery was filled with wounded soldiers. I was brought to the second floor."

From 22 to 30 December, the 1st Battalion of *Fallschirmjäger-Regiment 9* maintained its positions, which began west of Bei Antönchen, ran toward Faymonville north of the road, and then fell back to Waimes along the railway embankment, and finally ran toward Steinbach. Reconnaissance parties, assault parties, and counterattacks followed each other. Not even on Christmas Eve or on the holy days was there quiet at the front.

Modern view of the railroad line between Faymonville and
Weywertz. HANS WIJERS

Major Heinz Fick, commander of the 2nd Company of
Fallschirmjäger-Regiment 9, wrote to his wife: "On Christmas Eve,
with the enemy opposite us at about one kilometer from
Malmédy, after eight days I finally find the opportunity to write
you, my love.

"The losses in my company regrettably have been high but
with our assembled forces the enemy has to be overrun. We
gain a rich booty in cigarettes, tinned fruit, vehicles, and so on.
As our trains are not coming up, we have to live off the land.
Yesterday and today, we even managed to make some warm
food. Apart from that, we live on cakes and chocolate. Now
tomorrow is Christmas. Hopefully, the weather continues to
remain a mild winter and the enemy will concede himself
beaten soon. It is a pity that we only hear rumors about what is
going on at other sectors of the front. Hopefully, it is true that
our troops occupied Liege days ago and our tanks reached
Dunkirk. And that in an attack on Merseburg, 350 enemy
bombers were shot down.

"I sit in a detached house, in the cellar of which there are
two Walloon peasant wives with six small children. By day they

Heinz Fick.

often pray for hours. Around the house all has been plowed up by impact of shells, as the enemy has this location bore-sighted."

The war diary of the U.S. 1st Infantry Division contains the following for 23 December 1944: "Report from the U.S. V Corps: We finally got air [i.e., spotter planes were in the skies]! They are in the air now. Got targets; going to shoot at them: A column moves from Faymonville to Schoppen and another goes for Büllingen. Pass the word to your forward troops, as we want to know the results of the mission."

Oberschütze Rudi Frühbeisser of *Fallschirmjäger-Regiment 9* reports: "23 December 1944. In the morning, after a lengthy barrage, the platoon commander of the 2nd Company, Paul Frömmer, was caught by a direct hit on his hole.

"Today the population of Faymonville was evacuated by order! By 1100 hours, a transport of refugees left the town. On the road to Schoppen, the transport was spotted by the Americans and presumably taken for German transport. Therefore, the road leading to Schoppen was completely covered with intense artillery fire. The priest of Faymonville came up to our commander in a state of complete emotional breakdown and asked him to contact the Americans by radio and ask for a halt to the fire. This request for understandable reasons couldn't be granted.

"There are some losses among the inhabitants. In the afternoon, it starts again, how great, to snow. An ammunition truck driving to Faymonville is hit, when it wants to enter the place, by several grenades and begins to burn. The truck driver and his passenger, with the help of some volunteers, manage to bring the precious ammunition from the truck without damage. In the evening, the enemy artillery fire increases so heavily, that several houses are on fire. The enemy also fires several phosphorus grenades in town."

Josef Pfeiffer, ten years old at the time, experienced the horrible bombardment of the evacuated civilian population of Faymonville by the American artillery. With a few possessions, he, his father (August), and his mother had to move toward Schoppen. He recalls what he experienced: "All of a sudden, a German soldier entered our cellar and said: 'All have to leave, the entire village has to be evacuated.' There we went, father, mother and my little sister with two bicycles and me as a little boy. I had to move with the heavy bicycle, loaded with suitcases, etc. over an icy road towards Schoppen.

"A bit beyond, there was a toppled tree on the road and then I saw a dead German soldier. I stood still and looked at the dead man. I could not understand that people killed each other.

"And then high up at the cross the American artillery began to fire on us! My father cried 'Cover!' And when it stopped again he shouted 'Up!' This happened perhaps seven to ten times. I was still lying, and then I did not hear my father

Josef Pfeiffer (middle) with his father and mother. JOSEF PFEIFFER

cry 'On!' Then I began to cry. My father, a little forward in the road ditch saw me and blinked. It was good luck that he saw me. And the American artillery was firing continuously, the shrapnel was hissing all around us!

"Then I had to go on, but I couldn't anymore. My father said, 'Josef throw your bicycle in the ditch.' (After the war, I went there often to see whether I could still find my bicycle.) The ditches were full of people who were lying flat. On the road there were dead horses, a cart that had been turned over, suitcases that had fallen down left and right, etc. Then my father saw a German soldier at the edge of the woods and shouted, 'Josef, go to him into the hole!'

"Not long afterward, a shell landed close to the hole, and I began to pray. Then the German soldier shouted, 'Shut up, that doesn't help anyhow!' Then shrapnel came down from the treetops, branches fell on top of us, and the German soldier did not move anymore. Then my father shouted, 'Out of

The second of woods where Josf Pfeiffer sought cover. JOSEF PFEIFFER

the hole!' On the road there were two dead people, I don't know anymore who they were. Then my father shouted: 'Back! We can't go on forward!' The road in front of us was filled with shell craters. Then we went back. Walking and walking over the slick snow! And then on to the first house of Faymonville. We entered it and as soon as we were inside a German soldier shouted, 'Quickly down into the cellar; when the house takes a hit, the wall will come down on top of you!' Well, we had not even passed the last step, when a shell exploded near the house and just like the German soldier had just said, the wall came down. When we were in the cellar I looked to see whether I had been wounded, but noted that several pieces of shrapnel had gotten stuck in my clothing; they hadn't penetrated but were stuck in the leather."

Rudi Frühbeisser continues: "There were some losses among the inhabitants. In the afternoon it began to snow like mad once more. A munitions lorry, which was driving down to Faymonville, was hit by several shells the moment it entered the village and began to burn. A few volunteers came up to help the driver and co-driver unload the valuable ammunition from the lorry without any damage. By the evening the artillery fire increased to such an extent that several houses in the village began to burn. The Yanks also fired several phosphorous shells in to the village."

At 1538 hours, the 1st Infantry Division reported the following to V Corps: "The 16th Infantry Regiment has reported to the division that in front of its 2nd Battalion, enemy units north of Ondenval are moving in its direction. The estimated strength is 200 enemy soldiers with halftracks." At 2135, the 16th Infantry Regiment reported to the 1st Infantry Division: "A reconnaissance party of E Company has reached Steinbach down to the road, which runs underneath the railway line." At 2245, the 18th Infantry Regiment of the 1st Infantry Division reported that a patrol from F Company went from location 904026 west along the bank of the stream to the road crossing and ran into a road block just north of the woods; they were fired upon and went toward Schoppen were they met heavier and heavier fire until they reached coordinate 899016 where they turned back. They reported the road block and surrounding area was heavily booby-trapped. The 18th Infantry was told to have the 3rd Battalion reconnoiter tomorrow for routes by which to support the 16th Infantry.

The 1st Infantry Division's artillery reported that they had fired on a number of places during the previous night and during the day (24 December) as called for by infantry and air observation. These included the towns of Möderscheid, Schoppen, Faymonville, Steinbach, and Büllingen. Excellent results were observed, particularly in the town of Büllingen.

At 0045 hours on 24 December, the 16th Infantry reported: "Two enemy tanks and about 15 infantry came up to the road junction at coordinate 839012. As the enemy approached that point, we placed artillery, mortar and small arms fire on them. The enemy returned the fire and withdrew a little, but are still around. At 0310 hours, the 18th Infantry Regiment reported that a patrol from C Company had gone south to the edge of the woods and found an abandoned friendly gun position, but no personnel. The 16th Infantry

Regiment told Division Headquarters at 0325 hours that an enemy halftrack ran into the mine field in the E Company sector."

Frühbeisser of *Fallschirmjäger-Regiment 9* resumes his account: "24 December 1944. Total losses: 2 men, both wounded. Today is Christmas Eve! With many young privates it is the first Christmas they have to spend away from their parents' home. It is a very quiet morning. In the afternoon individual shells fall on the village. By 1945 hours, a strong artillery fire, machine gun and mortar fire sets in. The majority falls on the positions of the 1st Company under *Hauptmann* Schiffke.

"Since the later afternoon, the 1st Company, however, lies prepared in its blocking position to beat off a possible American attack. At the fall of darkness the Yanks carefully advance with little infantry in the area of the 1st Battalion. The Yanks, who are not wearing any snow camouflage, clearly stand out against the landscape. Everyone is lying in wait and awaits the order. Sights are fixed; weapons are loaded and prepared to fire. The screw tops on the bottom of the hand grenade grips are screwed off and the grenades are laid down ready to be thrown. Although everyone is trembling with excitement in the cold the fire discipline is maintained; not a shot leaves the barrel!

"About seventy meters in front of the positions the Yanks turn and go back again. In the bombardment that preceded this, the commander of the signals platoon of the 2nd Battalion, *Oberleutnant* Senkel, received a splinter wound in the upper thigh. Dispatch rider *Oberschütze* Bruno Linowitzki, who had been a part of the motorcycle platoon in Normandy, is hit by a barrage at a crossroads. When he doesn't return, the old sweats of the motorcycle platoon, *Obergefreiter* Harald Heisterkamp and *Obergefreiter* Franz Burger, two always-loyal Rhinelanders, go off to look for their *Oberschütze*. However, they only find his shattered and destroyed cycle and his briefcase. There is no trace at all of Linowitzki.

"By 2000 hours, the majority of the soldiers in the 1st Battalion area leave their positions by crawling to go to the warm cellars of the few houses that remain upright. Then every-where Christmas is celebrated, as soldiers should. Small Christmas trees are erected and partially decorated with Christmas decorations that have been found in the houses. With hoarse throats the Christmas song 'Silent Night' is started. The others, who have ended up in the command post of the 1st Company, join hesitantly. With the second line there is only humming, however, as no one can produce a tone anymore. Old and young paratroopers wipe their eyes with their calloused hands and think of home. Our commander, *Hauptmann* Fritz Schiffke, gives a short speech and wishes us a happy holiday. Then there is a wonderful punch, which our chef from Nürnberg, *Obergefreiter* Sepp Riegel, has managed to conjure up from somewhere. Also some good bottles of sekt, which have been found, are spent. Later that night, individual groups crawl to the positions with cigarettes and whisky to relieve the comrades in their trenches. As a surprise there has been mail shortly before the relief. The current staff sergeant, from an airbase unit of the air force and a coward and scared pants from the book, once more has ventured forward. We old paratroopers laugh in his face when he wants to tell us something in his barracks courtyard voice. Some of us have said before that if he only had a small part of our old *Feldwebel* Berthold Weitzke, he would have been usable. The night remains quiet."

On 25 December, *Hauptmann* Schiffke took over command of the 1st Battalion of *Fallschirmjäger-Regiment 9*, and *Oberstleutnant Freiherr* Schenk zu Schweinsberg took command of *Fallschirmjäger-Regiment 8*. Command of the 1st Company was taken over by *Oberleutnant* Strasser.

Rudi Frühbeisser continues his story: "25 December 1944—total losses: twelve men (three killed, nine wounded). By evening it happens! At dusk a slender figure approaches the command post of the 1st Company, which is located in the single house on a hill in the direction of Ruthier, after the railway crossing of Faymonville. Two old paratroopers, who are securing the house from the roadside immediately recognize this shape as the battalion commander, who is marching up there in boots, jump trousers and the thick sweater with a rolling collar and cap. A short, military report and the 'old one' signals them to rest. Some other units in the vicinity now also recognize the *Oberstleutnant* of the 1st Battalion in the man with the rolling collar. In our good, warm hut, he sits down with us and tells us: 'Guys, sadly I have to leave you!' One of us very unmilitary answers: 'Now you're joking!' But the *Oberstleutnant* says: 'I have been ordered to assume command of Parachute Regiment 8!' Now all mutiny. Then the lieutenant-colonel stands up and says: '*Hauptmann* Schiffke, I name you my successor and herewith hand you command of the 1st Battalion!' We congratulate our old captain; some even tap him on the shoulder. Therefore, *Hauptmann* Schiffke immediately promotes the little *Oberleutnant* Strasser to commander of the 1st Company. He says: 'Strasser, bring my few remaining soldiers whole through the fight, my old sweats all will support you!' Then our old battalion commander bids farewell with the words: 'So, now I immediately have to go to Schoppen, as the regimental command post of *Fallschirmjäger-Regiment 8* is located there!' All of us accompany our *Oberstleutnant* to the front of the house and our best wishes are shouted after him. *Hauptmann* Schiffke also grabs his things and goes off to the battalion command post, to assume command of the 1st Battalion.

"At 2200 hours, a very heavy artillery and mortar fire opens upon Faymonville and vicinity. *Obergefreiter* Ritter of the 2nd Battalion staff is killed in this. In the 8th Company, driver *Obergefreiter* Füreder is killed, and in the 6th Company, *Obergefreiter* Lehnert is killed.

Hauptmann Heinz Fick, commander of 2nd Company of *Fallschirmjäger-Regiment 9*, wrote to his wife: "According to the date, today is the second day of Christmas, but for those of us who are directly opposite the enemy, there hardly has been any Christmas. Snow fell, and from a nearby village the company cook sent cakes and poultry, furthermore I could hand out four Iron Crosses, 2nd Class, and announce some promotions to *Oberschütze*. Apart from that there are no indications of the festive season here. By day, my boys lie in their earth holes for

All across the European theater, American troops receive Christmas presents, some in their foxhole and others in Paris. U.S. ARMY

twelve hours and can only be relieved at night, because otherwise the Yanks would immediately report in with mortar, rifle and machine gun fire. I am sitting in the cellar of a house with my company and cannot see the future with confidence.

Ludwig Havighorst of the 15th Company, *Fallschirmjäger-Regiment 9.*
FRANK RIESER

"Unfortunately, in our sector the Americans have reinforced themselves so much, that our advance has stalled completely. Hopefully, things work out better in the other sectors,
so that we can regain our movement once more."

As with all three regiments and divisional units in these
Christmas days, fresh replacements—"refreshments"—took
place. The depleted ranks were filled up with inexperienced
paratroopers of *Fallschirm-Ersatz- und Ausbildungs-Regiment 3*
(Paratroop Replacement and Training Regiment 3). Further
reinforcements took place via certain redistribution. In this
way, the 1st Battalion of *Fallschirmjäger-Regiment 9* received
comrades of the 15th Pioneer Company of *Oberleutnant*
Havighorst and even from the 2nd Company of *Fallschirm-
Panzerjäger-Abteilung 3* (Parachute Antitank Battalion 3) of

Leonhardt Maniura.

Major Härtle. After the "refreshments" were distributed, the 1st Battalion still had only 9 officers and 321 men.

Obergefreiter Leonhardt Maniura of the 15th Pioneer Company of *Fallschirmjäger-Regiment 9* recalls: "One day after the beginning of the Ardennes offensive was my eighteenth birthday. My platoon had remained behind as operational reserve in Weiden (near Cologne). Exactly on Christmas Day 1944, we were ordered to move toward Amel. We were transported by truck to Euskirchen, which was rather destroyed. We continued, more or less on lorries—I seem to remember driving a trailer!—partially on foot to Stadtkyll, Prüm, and via St. Vith to Amel. It was two or three days before we reached Amel. Here in the falling dusk we looked for our company command post and trains, as our rucksacks with fresh laundry, etc., were with them. We were shouting round the area; troops from various units reported in, but none from our unit. Finally, we got a hint that in one of the bigger buildings in front of the town, to the left of the St. Vith road, far in front of Amel, a command post was located; it was our unit. The first question was what had taken us so long? As if it was so easy to travel down from Weiden!

"Here lay much snow, and we helped putting snow chains onto trucks. Here we also learned that our unit already had suffered many losses – I seem to remember, nearly half – and that they were glad we had turned up as reinforcements. Artillery fire came up all the way to here and it was continuous, so that the front lines could not be far away. We were billeted in single houses in Amel, but had to hand in our machine guns, as ammunition was scarce, and received carbines. We celebrated New Year's Eve in our billets (roughly opposite the filling station) on the water tap. In Amel there was more American military material lying around that we had seen on the way up; we also saw a downed American Lightning (fighter-bomber)—to the right next to the main road—toward St. Vith, close to Amel."

Hauptmann Heinz Fick, commander of 2nd Company of *Fallschirmjäger-Regiment 9*, wrote to his wife: "I had to stop writing this letter yesterday, as our house, which contained sixteen of us in the cellar, was put alight by shelling. The Americans are peppering our entire sector with phosphorous shells, and a gun has taken up position about one kilometer from us, which is firing at us over open sights. After *Oberleutnant* Later, who had been assigned to me in early December, had been taken out by a wound on 17 December; I now was given a twenty-four-year-old director of music as platoon commander. In the meantime all my old and experienced soldiers have been killed or wounded here. Now I have only half the company I had in November, so that by now everybody has to fend for two. Thank God we could move back into our cellar, which could be heated, after we had doused energetically."

Rudi Frühbeisser again: "26 December 1944—total losses: three men (one killed, two wounded). In a barrage at dawn, *Schütze* Siemon of the 7th Company is mortally wounded in the shoulder. In the afternoon for the first time since some days,

Rolf Odendahl.

more than once a V-1 comes flying. As soon as the flying vehicle reaches the American positions everyone opens up with all weapons. From a recently captured issue of the American soldier paper *Stars and Stripes,* our comrades who know English read to us about the very heavy destruction caused in London by V-1s and V-2s. Also the artillery spotter shows himself in the skies once more. Apart from this, the day in the entire regimental area goes by without any larger disturbances."

To the right of the 1st Battalion of *Fallschirmjäger-Regiment 9,* elements of *Fallschirmjäger-Regiment 8* had to be inserted into the line since *Fallschirmjäger-Regiment 5* also had suffered considerable losses.

Platoon commander Rolf Odendahl of the 1st Company, *Fallschirmjäger-Regiment 5,* remembers: "I spent Christmas 1944 in Meyerode. My company commander and I had a breakdown of our truck on the way to the Ardennes, and got stuck in the village of Lissendorf in the Eifel. On 21 December, we marched with now newly arrived soldiers at the front, first to Meyerode behind the frontline, which was intended as a rallying point for the unit. Parts of the company, which were employed at the front, were supposed to move there for a rest and to re-collect. Because of the completely clogged streets, our truck did not come through and we made the largest part of the route walking.

"We must have arrived in Meyerode on 22 or 23 December and took lodging in a restaurant. The landlord and landlady were still in the house! Since no supplies arrived because of blocked roads and we had nothing to eat, I went with three men on the hunt and shot a deer with my carbine in the forest. I grazed it with a pocket knife, and the other hid it under a pine tree, which we then use as a Christmas tree. An American *Jabo* was shot down over us and we went to the crash site, where a lieutenant requested statements from us as witnesses of the launch. On 24 December, I dressed the deer and cooked goulash for us. Shortly before, our comrades, who were previously on the front in Faymonville, came back from the front. They were located in a mill and found plenty of flour, so that we could bake. At the same time a supply truck came by and brought food and Christmas packages. So we suddenly had plenty to eat. I left the civilians who had nothing to eat. Therefore the deer ragout.

"We spent the Christmas days in Meyerode. On 27 December, our company commander was called away with *Leutnant* Roth, his second officer, and *Oberleutnant* Helmut Schwarzendahl (platoon leader) to discuss the attack on Faymonville. On the way back, the car was attacked by a Jabo at Mon Antone. Roth and the battalion commander, *Major* Willibald Jost, were killed by shell fragments. *Oberleutnant* Schwarzendahl had gone back to walk because he had a bad feeling about the road. He was an experienced front-line soldier and must have had an inkling. He took over the leadership of the company.

"On 26 or 27 December—I can't remember the exact date anymore—my company would be committed to an attack on

Hauptmann Siegfried Platz, commander of 3rd Battalion, *Fallschirmjäger-Regiment 5*, killed on 29 December. FRANK RIESER

an American position at Faymonville. I was ordered to carry out an attack with my platoon on an American position across a plain of 300 meters devoid of cover.

"First, there was a down slope, and then it rose again. There was much snow, but there was no other cover. It was known only that the Americans had cited two heavy machine guns. I had said goodbye to life, as I thought the entire operation was hopeless.

"The start of the attack should begin when the *12th SS-Panzer-Division 'Hitlerjugend'*, which was to attack Bütgenbach, had reached this location. In the meantime the Americans spotted our preparations and covered us with an intense artillery barrage, which inflicted considerable losses on us.

"As the attack of the *12th SS* on Bütgenbach failed with heavy losses, our attack was cancelled, and we moved all the way back to Schoppen, where we spent New Year's Eve."

Before Christmas the 2nd and 3rd Companies of the 1st Battalion of *Fallschirmjäger-Regiment 9* were moved to the left flank of the regiment, namely to Thirimont. In this way, the 3rd Battalion—which could cover only the heights of Farm Grosbois, Freyneux, the houses "at the cross," and the terrain toward Remonval with pockets—received the necessary reinforcements. On New Year's Eve, the fighting elements of the 1st Battalion were reinforced from the 2nd Company of *Hauptmann* Heinz Fick and the 3rd Company of *Hauptmann* Woitscheck and with smaller elements of the 2nd and 3rd Companies of *Fallschirmjäger-Regiment 9* and moved back to Faymonville in the night of 1 January 1945.

Gefreiter Max Strobel of the 1st Battalion recalls: "I will not forget this march, because at 2400 hours at midnight the Americans fired off twelve red flares. Shortly afterward, our mortars fired on houses north of Thirimont, where the Yanks lay, in order to prevent an attack being launched from there."

Hauptmann Fick writes: "Exactly as on Christmas Eve, where we had to change positions in the night of 25 December, we were on the move in the night of New Year's Eve. I had to hand over my entire sector, and certainly did not regret it as we were in a rather dangerous corner under direct enemy fire. The march through the enchanting winter landscape of the wide Venn by night, with full moon, and in addition through snow topped woods, for me was very impressive, after one had spent about 250 hours mainly in cellars. On 1 January, under the orders of the director of music assigned to me, my company took up new positions, while on 2 January I went to see a specialist doctor because of an intestinal disturbance which had been plaguing me for the past fourteen days."

Back in Faymonville, this *Kampfgruppe* and elements of the 2nd and 3rd Companies moved to individual buildings, which lay slightly to the north outside Faymonville. Only by 10–11 January 1945, the positions of *Fallschirmjäger-Regiment 9* in and

The Möderscheider mill, headquarters of *3rd Fallschirmjäger-Division* and *Fallschirmjäger-Regiment 9*.

around Thirimont were reinforced by the 1st and 4th Companies of the 1st Battalion. The main dressing station of the 1st Battalion moved location one or two days later.

Oberschütze Walter Wittlinger of the staff of 2nd Battalion remembers: "On Christmas Eve, before the onset of darkness, we were once more committed to Faymonville. Already during our advance over snow covered fields (not visible to the enemy) again and again mortars put down harassing fire on our way. We suffered our first losses when we entered Faymonville. The battalion command post was set up in the cellar of the vestry next to the church. We had petroleum lamps for light. I can remember that petrol mixed with cooking salt was used instead of petroleum. Here is where we had to settle down.

"On 25 December, I had to return to Schoppen with a comrade to hand in the strength report to the regiment. Here we ran into civilians who had been evacuated from Faymonville. An elderly woman asked us whether it was possible to bring a large bucket with boiled and salted meat from a certain house in Faymonville back for her. We could not show ourselves on the road from Faymonville to Schoppen, as this was under American observation for long stretches. And we had to cover this road around midday.

"Between Christmas and New Year's, the regimental command post was moved back to the monastery of Montenau, about five to six kilometers south of Faymonville. For us this road was far more dangerous and problematical. As mentioned before, the report to the regiment always had to be handed in around midday. This was the time that the American artillery was active."

CHAPTER 8

Events in the Operational Area of Elements of *Fallschirmjäger-Regiment 5* and *Fallschirmjäger-Regiment 8*

The border between *Fallschirmjäger-Regiment 5* and *Fallschirmjäger-Regiment 8* was located at Weiler Mon Antöne or Bei Antönchen. Since 18 December, the 1st Battalion of *Fallschirmjäger-Regiment 8*, under *Major* Bruno Krohs, had been at the front at the railway station of Oberweywertz, which is located at the Bütgenbach–Waimes road. The battalion command post was in the detached house Houtenborn in the area north of Schoppen. During the period from 18 to 20 December, *Schütze* Lohmann and *Oberschütze* Klimmsek went missing there. *Leutnant* Büchner at first was division liaison officer of the *3rd Fallschirmjäger-Division*. Therefore, he knew that the station of Oberweywertz and the Bütgenbach–Waimes road on 18–19 December was in the hands of the 1st Battalion of *Fallschirmjäger-Regiment 8*. On Wednesday, 20 December, the 3rd Battalion of *Fallschirmjäger-Regiment 8* was relieved. In the middle of this relief, an attack was launched by American troops. In this action between Stellwerk and the Oberweywertz station, thirty-four paratroopers were captured.

Leutnant Bruno Büchner, a company commander in the 1st Battalion of *Fallschirmjäger-Regiment 8*, remembers: "First, I was liaison officer with *Generalmajor* Wadehn at the division command post in the mill in Möderscheid. Shortly before Christmas in Schoppen, I took over command of a company. It

was a grab-bag of men; it even contained a Knight's Cross
bearer of the *Luftwaffe*. The relief in Marienhof took place
under heavy mortar fire, and many units—young soldiers—
were sacrificed here. The relieving company itself was at the
end of its tether. The Yanks were firing from Elsenborn; we
really were cannon-fodder here!"

Büchner changed the trace of the main frontline. The outpost of Stellwerk on the left side was housed in an earthen
bunker in a fir wood. Mrs. Wismes and her three little children
had to leave Marienhof. The paratroopers of *Fallschirmjäger-
Regiment 8* and the relieving *Fallschirmjäger-Regiment 5* retained
an unsavory memory of Stellwerk and the Oberweywertz railway station.

The success of the frontline change became clear the next
evening: no more losses at Stellwerk. Prior to the change,
almost every night three to five American soldiers, coming
from Oberweywertz, were captured after attacking with hand
grenades and sub-machine guns.

In the *3rd Fallschirmjäger-Division*'s sector, a major regroup-
ing took place beginning January 1945. While *Fallschirmjäger-
Regiment 5* mainly remained in the Büllingen–Bütgenbach
area, *Fallschirmjäger-Regiment 8* took up positions on the
Klingelsberg (hilly wooded section) to Bütgenbach and in
Faymonville, while the 1st Battalion of *Fallschirmjäger-Regiment
9*, southwest of the town of Waimes, was moved forward
near the Baugnez area. In the front line of *Fallschirmjäger-Regiment 8*, its 1st Battalion was on the left, its 3rd Battalion in the
Ondenval–Remonval–Freyneux area, while its 2nd Battalion
held the area from Remonval via Steinbach to Faymonville, the
(current) command post of *Fallschirmjäger-Regiment 8*.

In the first days of the New Year, it was relatively quiet at
the front. However, daily harassing fire by the Americans
brought losses. Also at the edge of the woods of the Bütgenbacher Heck, elements of *Fallschirmjäger-Regiment 5* had taken
up position and, after further heavy losses, were at the end of
their strength. The Bütgenbacher Heck–Schoppen area
passed over to the defense.

Modern view of the Oberweywertz station. HANS WIJERS

Platoon commander Rolf Odendahl of the 1st Company of *Fallschirmjäger-Regiment 5* recollects: "On 1 January 1945, we were committed to the front line in the Bütgenbacher Heck area, at the edge of a forest track which formed the border between two divisions. There was a lot of snow, and we were housed in a earthen bunker built by the Americans. My platoon was barely over squad strength. With that we were supposed to hold several hundred meters of the frontline. My platoon consisted partly of senior sergeants and sergeants of the *Luftwaffe*, who were used as riflemen without any infantry training. One *Stabsfeldwebel*—a former fighter pilot and Knight's Cross bearer—was used as machine gunner. In my position was a *Leutnant* forward observer for the artillery. Because of the lack of ammunition, he only had two rounds available to fix the locations of blocking barrages in case of an attack. By day we could see the Americans walk around on the slopes opposite us, but were not allowed to fire. Only in an emergency were we permitted to fire.

"Next to me there was a company of elderly *Volksgrenadiers,* led by a *Hauptmann*, with whom I established contact. This captain told me, 'You have to do it all by yourself,' pointing to a soldier who was chopping some wood nearby, making a hell of a noise. He shouted, 'Hey you!' and the soldier turned his head and said, 'What, what did you say?' and the *Hauptmann* turned his face to me and said, 'This is the kind of soldiers I have to keep the lines with.' Because of the lack of soldiers, our front line consisted of only two light machine guns and two advanced slit trenches. We depended on the dense fir woods and the high snow to save us from penetrations. Sadly, this was in vain, as the soldiers of the U.S. 1st Infantry Division in broad daylight and by night penetrated our lines. On 3 January, we lost battalion commander *Oberleutnant* Hermann Wildbrett and company commander *Oberleutnant* Paul Kruchen and *Hauptfeldwebel* Heinz Emmer behind our lines.

"I had great luck, as an American barely missed me from two meters distance. He hit just a pocket of my *Knochensack* ["bag of bones," as the jump suit of the paratroopers was

Rolf Odendahl (right) talks with the author at Bütgenbacher Heck.

called]. I only cheated death because, according to the orders of my company commander, I collected food for my platoon at the company command post, took it to my earthen bunker and took cover in the hole. The attackers were wearing white camouflage clothing and could not be distinguished from our own troops. Therefore, I shouted at the shooter: 'You idiot, can't you tell you're firing at your own men?' Then it suddenly became clear to me that it was an American, and I used his astonishment about my shouting to dive into my hole."

Oberschütze Rudi Frühbeisser of *Fallschirmjäger-Regiment 9* reports: "5 January 1945. Since the early hours of the morning, heavy artillery and mortar fire came down on the town of Faymonville. Great care was warranted. At the 3rd Company, located in the village of Thirimont, *Schütze* Beck was killed. In Ondenval, *Obergefreiter* Günther Beck of the 15th Company was mortally hit by a piece of shrapnel in the head."

Lissendorf cemetery (Germany).

Leonhardt Maniura of the 15th Pioneer Company, *Fallschirmjäger-Regiment 9*, writes: "On 5 January, about 0500 hours in the morning, a shell exploded in our quarters, at the windowsill of the room in which we were lying. On the evening before, my friend Günther Beck told Walter Hansch (the three of us were the only Silesians in the company), who was lying rather close to the door in the living room, 'Walter, stand up and let Leo sleep close by the door. You know that he always wakes us up at night with his walks to the bog.' And so we exchanged positions. When the shell exploded, my friend Günther Beck (Senior Lance Corporal) got a piece of shrapnel through the top of the skull, which we could not see right away. After we had freed ourselves from the destroyed room, we brought the nearly unconscious man to the cellar, and I immediately ran off to fetch a medic billeted in the house beyond this farm, in the platoon command post on the road to Vieux-Mühle, about 100 meters distant.

"I got out of breath, often having to stop for a minute, but made it and got back with the medic. In the cellar we saw that

Leonhardt Maniura and his friend Walter Hän-sch, who was killed on 5 January 1945. L. MANIURA

we could no longer be of any help. I was amazed that my friend Günther Beck was murmuring 'Hail Mary', as he was a protestant. After a while the medic thought he was dead and used a feather, holding it in front of his nose. No result. I remembered that one can establish the death of a human by sticking a needle underneath a finger nail. The medic did not know this. We tried it, but he did not jerk.

"Now we looked for my other friend, *Schütze* Walter Hän-sch, and had a suspicion that he had run off in a panic. But then we found him lying dead in the room. I had the good fortune that shelves had partially protected me; the other comrades had gotten away clean. Someone got hold of a horse-drawn sled, and as a friend I was allowed to take both

The house (number 34) at Ondenval where both friends died after a shell hit it.

dead men to the company command post at Amel, where they were buried. In Amel we buried both at the cemetery to the right of the main road in the center of the cemetery (about at the spot where now the grave of 'Schommers' is located).

"After this, in Ondenval, we changed quarters and ended up as the smallest little band in a house to the right of the main road at the entrance to the village, in front of the church. One night I saw—even though it was barely a new moon—about three or four meters in front of me, coming downhill on the main road, a group of soldiers in white camouflage marching past in the deep snow, entering the town. They did not see me. I wanted to give them a shout, but was too lazy to do it. The next morning, I found out that it had been an American reconnaissance party!"

CHAPTER 9

D-Day in Belgium, 13 January 1945

During the German counteroffensive, the *1st SS-Panzer-Division* had reached the area of Trois-Ponts, Stavelot, and Stoumont–La Gleize. But when the initiative passed to the U.S. troops in the Ardennes salient, what remained of the *1st SS-Panzer-Division* was withdrawn and replaced by second-rate infantry units. The sector held by the *18th Volksgrenadier-Division*, under the command of *Oberst* Günther Hoffmann-Schönborn (this unit had been fighting at the start of the offensive in the Schnee Eifel, capturing St. Vith and large parts of the U.S. 106th Infantry Division), was east from the Salm River at Trois-Ponts to Baugnez.

The *18th Volksgrenadier-Division* controlled its new frontline positions with two regiments. The strength of the two regiments was estimated at 800 troops. *Grenadier-Regiment 294*, under the command of *Oberstleutnant* Wilhelm Drüke, controlled the west part, but had to give up Wanne and Spineux on 7 January. *Grenadier-Regiment 293*, under the command of *Oberstleutnant Witte*, was on the right side of *Grenadier-Regiment 294*, and its line of defense was stretched out to the crossroads of Baugnez. In immediate reserve was *Grenadier-Regiment 295*. The regiment suffered heavy losses. Since 24 December, it had been under the command of *Oberstleutnant* Klimke. On 4 January near Abrefontaine, both commanders of the 2nd Battalion, *Hauptmann* Folz and *Hauptmann* Winterberg were missing. On 12 January 1945, the third battalion commander, *Hauptmann* Huber, also went missing near Logbiermé.

Since the Battle of the Bulge started, the strength of the *18th Volksgrenadier-Division* had gone down to about half. In immediate reserve were a conjectured 1,600 additional men from the following units attached or otherwise in support: the Field Replacement Battalion, the Füsilier and Alarm Company, the Engineer Battalion, the 434th Construction Battalion, and OT Blomberg (Division Combat School). Only *Artillery-Regiment 1818*, with about 1,700 men (including the 87th Nebelwerfer Regiment) under the command of *Oberstleutnant* Friedrich Hadenfeldt and *Pioneer-Bataillon 1818* under the command of *Hauptmann* Kuhr were still up to nearly its full strength. These units were capable of being employed as infantry. That made a total of 4,000 men that could possibly have been employed on the U.S. 30th Infantry Division's front.

The 1818th Tank Destroyer Unit, under the command of *Hauptmann* Günther Rennhack, had only three tank destroyers and five antitank guns and was kept in reserve behind *Volksgrenadier-Regiment 293*. From 12 January, the *18th Volksgrenadier-Division*'s headquarters was located near the crossroads of Kaiserbaracke. However, that was not an integrated fighting force, but a scattered attempt to fuse a number of unrelated units into an effective force. That those so-called "scattered forces" proved determined, difficult to defeat, and dealt the 30th Infantry Division an extremely large number of casualties, will be quickly evident in the account that follows.

Furthermore, it was known that behind this line the area was occupied by strong elements of the *3rd Fallschirmjäger-Division*, which had been in the area since the start of the Ardennes offensive, and since that time moved to make a strong defense line roughly south of the road between Bütgenbach and Malmédy, including the towns of Faymonville, Weywertz, Thirimont, Schoppen, and others and all the surrounding hills, that would prove to be a hard nut to crack.

The terrain in the area and the obstacles it presented were essentially the same as the area the 30th Infantry Division had been fighting in since December. The heavily wooded areas and the protection and tactical advantage they offered defending troops must be remembered while considering this operation. Further, it must be kept in mind the condition of the road net. Snow had fallen in the Ardennes region almost every day since shortly before Christmas 1944. After some three weeks, high drifts had formed on both sides of every road. If the route was a fairly well traveled one, it had become slick as ice. Lanes leading to points of vantage in a dominating piece of terrain were hidden by the drifts, and to gain such ground was possible only by slugging up the forward slope and knocking the enemy off.

Fortunately, there were no great hampering bodies of water between the American forces' line of departure and the final objective. The L'Ambléve River, farther to the west, crossed the U.S. zone, running from west to east near Ligneuville. It was not considered an obstacle of any large proportion for though it was a swift flowing river, it was only two to three feet deep at critical crossing points. Branches of it were so narrow that they were tactically inconsequential.

One of the biggest obstacles was of course, the weather and the effect it had on the physical condition of the men. Though every advantage was taken of shelters of any type, and a steady policy of rotating companies within a battalion was followed, the men were frequently wet and cold for long periods of time, often for more than a day. The rate of frostbite was high, though the number of trench foot cases was remarkably low.

At the beginning of January, the American units on the entire front between Thirimont–Schoppen–Bütgenbach–Waimes were given the order to advance against the German forces. The reconnaissance unit of the 16th Infantry Regiment of the 1st Infantry Division, part of a combat group, was moved toward Weywertz (the units were located in resting positions in Robertville and surrounding villages) and launched their attack from there.

The weather was cold, and there was deep snow, which hampered the American advance considerably. The reinforced American 23rd Infantry Regiment of the 2nd Infantry Division, with elements of the 741st Tank Battalion, was to attack south from Waimes. Farther to the west were elements of the 30th Infantry Division charged with pushing the enemy out of Thirimont and surrounding villages.

Oberschütze Rudi Frühbeisser of *Fallschirmjäger-Regiment 9* records: "11 January 1945. In a scouting party consisting of a squad of the 8th Company in the area in front of Faymonville, *Schütze* Paul Kreit was captured. The current front in this area ran as follows: the road from Waimes to Baugnez was no-man's-land. So in the last night we strolled down no-man's-land, bypassing Thirimont to Ondenval–Remonval–Steinbach –Faymonville–Antönchen. The first-aid post of the 1st Battalion of *Fallschirmjäger-Regiment 9* was located in Thirimont in the village street on the left side next to a small repair shop for motorcycle wheels. In the house next to the first-aid post, a squad of the 15th Pioneer Company of *Oberleutnant* Havighorst, with *Stabsfeldwebel* Schulze, had taken up residence. The house was turned into a tiny depot. At dusk the soldiers laid down a belt of mines south of Thirimont for protection.

During the entire night of 11–12 January, American artillery fire came down on Thirimont. On the morning of 12 January, after the artillery fire died down a bit, *Hauptmann* Schiffke went to the mayor and ordered him to leave the town with its inhabitants immediately. Before dusk all the civilians began leaving the town.

The original plan of the American command, though an unexpected amount of enemy resistance caused changes to be made, called for the 119th Infantry Regiment, 30th Infantry Division, to seize Hedomont two hours prior to H-hour and then continue south and capture Bellevaux and Lamonriville and establish bridgeheads at Pont. On the left of the 119th Infantry Regiment, the 120th Infantry Regiment was to seize Huyer, Ligneuville, Haute Sarts, and Thirimont. That was expected to be the first phase, during which the 117th Infantry Regiment was to remain in reserve. It was then to attack to the south of the area taken by the 119th Infantry Regiment.

CHAPTER 10

The Battle for Bellevaux and Hedomont

The first day, 13 January 1945, was the most costly for the 30th Infantry Division, and an explanation is valuable for the picture it portrays of the type of German reaction encountered on the main line of enemy resistance.

At 0600 hours on 13 January, the American 119th Infantry Regiment, under the command of Col. R. A. Baker, attacked south for its objectives of Bellevaux and Hedomont. Pushing south from the outskirts of Malmédy at 0600 hours, the 3rd Battalion reached the northern edge of Hedomont by 0735 hours, where it was halted by extremely strong resistance.

That city, it will be remembered, was to be captured before 0800 hours, so that it would form a base for a push farther south. As the situation turned out, Hedomont was not taken by darkness of the same day. Supported by a company of tanks of the 743rd Tank Battalion, the 3rd Battalion, 119th Infantry Regiment, reached a point where mines damaged several tanks and held up the armor. The infantry received very heavy fire from the crest (500 meters) of the hill about 100 yards north of Hedomont. The infantry regrouped and with L Company striking out of the woods at the west side of the city and I Company attacking from the northeast, some gain was made. But in mid-afternoon, the firepower of the defending troops drove the 3rd Battalion back.

The 1st Battalion attacked Hedomont at 0730 hours to support the unsuccessful 3rd Battalion. Advancing to the northern edge of the city, it could make no more progress than the 3rd battalion. One platoon of tanks, supported by a

platoon of infantry from B Company, attempted to edge into
the city from the west side but were turned back with heavy
losses.

Chalas E. Mirick of H Company, 119th Infantry Regiment,
30th Infantry Division, remembers: "We jumped off somewhere in Belgium. About 0700 hours, a driver named Steard,
with the 743rd Tank Battalion, in a white tank dozer with a
grater blade on it, stuck his head out of the tank and asked if
anyone was from Kentucky. I told him I was from Pikeville and
he said he was from Manchester. We moved out around 0730
hours. We were on a steep and narrow road when we were
pinned down and not able to move. A lot of men were hit by
sniper and mortar fire. When some of the tanks started moving up the road they ran over some of the wounded and dead;
some were Germans. We took some prisoners, and if any of
them were wearing anything GI, we stripped them down to
their long johns, including the boots, and sent them back to
the rear. About 1000 hours, my squad leader, Cheatham R.
Hutchings, was hit in the face with mortar fire."

By 1800 hours, a definite penetration of the city had not
been made at any point and L, K, and I Companies of the 3rd
Battalion, plus B Company of the 1st Battalion, were in position around the northern side of the city. A and C Companies
were withdrawn to the north as regimental reserve.

In a letter of instruction dated 2000 hours on 13 January,
the 119th Infantry Regiment was directed to take Hedomont
that same night. From 2200 to 2230 hours, Hedomont
received a terrific artillery barrage, at the conclusion of which
I Company, under Capt. George D. Rehkopf, again attacked
from the east and L Company, led by Capt. Lawrence J.
Gaglioane, from the west, with K Company coming down from
the north. Stunned to some extent by the terrific barrage, and
the intensity of the infantry drive, the enemy fell back slowly
and stubbornly, and by 0320 hours on 14 January, the 3rd Battalion was in possession of the city.

During the first day's offensive, the 2nd Battalion of the
119th Infantry did not experience the difficulty the other two
battalions of the regiment encountered. At 0600 hours, the

Murray S. Pulver.

2nd Battalion moved off from its line of departure, and keeping in the cover of the wooded area, advanced 2,500 yards. By 0800 hours, they were on the outskirts of the city of Bellevaux, but received scattered fire from enemy elements occupying portions of buildings. Throughout the day fire fights occurred in the city, and at night fall, tiny enemy pockets were still present. At last light, G, F, and E Companies occupied positions from west to east, about 600 yards north of the city proper.

So much for the western part of the 30th Infantry Division attack on 13 January. It was the eastern portion that turned out to be so costly and even more difficult to penetrate.

Captain Murray S. Pulver, commander of B Company, 1st Battalion, 120th Infantry Regiment, 30th Infantry Division, writes: "Finally, on 13 January 1945, 'D-Day' began for us in Belgium. At 8 A.M. on that day, the 30th and the 1st Infantry

Divisions attacked the northern part of the Bulge to pinch off the German thrust.

"The 2nd Battalion moved toward Thirimont on our left; the 3rd Battalion attacked through Hedomont with Huyer and Hill 541 as their objectives; and our battalion in the center aimed for Géromont and 'Five Points' (Baugnez Crossroads).

"We encountered little resistance until we got close to 'Five Points'. Heavy fire then broke out lasting for a few minutes until the enemy realized the strength of our attacking forces and retreated.

"B Company now held a position south of 'Five Points'. On our right the 3rd Battalion took Hill 541 after a stiff fight. The 2nd Battalion fought its way to the outskirts of Thirimont where it was stopped by heavy machine gun and mortar fire. Some elements of the battalion had to withdraw from their exposed positions as enemy strength increased."

In the vicinity of the Baugnez Crossroads, elements of the 1st Battalion of *Volksgrenadier-Regiment 293* of the *18th Volksgrenadier-Division* were captured by men of the 1st Battalion, 120th Infantry Regiment. The commander of the 1st Battalion, *Hauptmann* Hartrampf, was missing since 13 January.

German resistance to the advance of the battalion was stiff, but the battalion seized its objective at 1000 hours. Throughout the whole day, German artillery was heavy in this sector.

Because of the heavy resistance encountered by the others, the 1st Battalion, 120th Infantry Regiment, did not continue forward; instead, A Company set up outposts at the "Five Points," while B Company was positioned in defense of Géromont. At noon, the commanding officer of the 1st Battalion was ordered to prepare plans for a night attack on Thirimont. The regimental command post moved from Beverce to Montbijou in the morning, and as evening came on, plans were completed for the seizure of Thirimont and "Haute Sarts" the next day. Because it had ample time to study the details of the operation, the 1st Battalion made sure that each man was thoroughly oriented and knew his exact duties.

CHAPTER 11

The Battle for Huyer

On the right flank, near Malmédy, the 3rd Battalion of the 120th Infantry Regiment was to attack the height of Huyer southwest of Baugnez. The 2nd Battalion was to advance from the direction of Waimes and take the town of Thirimont and the heights of "Hauts Sarts" south of it. The 1st Battalion was to remain in reserve, until the other battalions had attained their main objectives, and then it was to prepare to take Ligneuville. Accordingly, on the night of 12 January 1945, the 2nd Battalion moved to Waimes.

Tech Sergeant A. P. Wiley of the 2nd Platoon, M Company, 120th Infantry Regiment, 30th Infantry Division, recalls: "M Company was a heavy weapons company consisting of two heavy machine gun platoons and one 81mm mortar platoon. I was assigned to the 2nd Platoon (heavy machine guns) and the platoon sergeant was T/Sgt. Charles 'Red' Fredricks.

"We remained in our positions until the evening of 12 January and then moved to an assembly area south of Malmédy, attached to K Company. At 0800 hours, we jumped off and moved down the road toward a road junction called 'Five Points' [Baugnez]. We met little or no opposition, and as we moved to 'Five Points,' we discovered the bodies of some one hundred fifty or two hundred [actually eight-six] American soldiers who had been captured by the Germans and later rounded up in a field and machine-gunned. This was later referred to as the 'Malmédy Massacre.' All of the bodies were partially covered by snow, so we really did not know the full extent of what we had seen."

On schedule at 0800 hours, both battalions struck. Deep snow slowed the advancing units, and tanks and tank destroyers were useless.

Wiley continues: "We moved east of Hedomont toward Huyer and the high ground just beyond Huyer, designated as Hill 541. We were having a difficult time advancing through the deep snow when we encountered some small arms fire from the woods in front of us. We continued to move forward at a slow pace towards the dense woods returning the fire. As we came closer to the woods the enemy resistance became more stubborn causing us to have a few casualties."

The 3rd Battalion's plan was a "pincer" on a small scale. K Company, with tanks attached, was to attack between Hedomont and Géromont from the northwest of Huyer, while L Company was to strike south from the vicinity of "Five Points," both to meet upon the high ground. Echeloned to the left rear of K Company, I Company would move between the lead companies, clearing out Géromont and bypassed pockets en route. The plan looked perfect, but the minute the attack began, things did not go well. The two lead companies met withering small arms fire. I Company moved out, and desiring to gain contact with K Company, swung more and more to the right. After clearing Géromont, I Company continued 300 to 400 yards, still without contacting K Company. A sudden wall of small-arms resistance met the I Company riflemen as they trudged through the knee-deep snow towards Huyer. Members of the lead platoon heard their commander, whose name was 1st Lt. Tom F. Andrew, yell "Keep moving," just before he fell dead, a victim of enemy automatic fire. Thus began the most furious period of battle that day for I Company. Clumsy in the deep snow, tired and partially disorganized, the men could not escape the merciless fire of German weapons.

K and L Company were likewise held up and suffering a similar struggle. The casualties sustained by all three companies reached a new high. I Company was still unable to contact K Company on the right (west), but pushed on alone. Into the Huyer thickets, it forged its way, hampered by Germans concealed in the woods on its left flank, cleaning out an area as it could and reaching at last the hilltop. There the men looked around at each other and realized they now made up a force no bigger than a strong platoon. Still undaunted, the men pushed forward to take the remainder of the high ground, further south, overlooking Ligneuville. Suddenly came much firing to I Company's right rear, and soon the sounds were discovered to emanate from a platoon of K Company, led by Lieutenant Sheen, which was struggling with an enemy force. The remainder of K Company was still battling far behind, and the I Company platoon joined with that from K Company to continue the drive forward. The two platoons made an advance of 1000 yards, overcoming a German patrol and reaching within 500 yards of German artillery pieces. Then, at 1500 hours, word reached the group that K and L Companies had gained the main heights of Huyer, and that the remainder of I Company was to return there, leaving the K Company platoon on outpost.

A. P. Wiley concludes: "Finally, around 1500 hours, we made it to high ground overlooking the town of Ligneuville, and we dug in. Our platoon had one man wounded from the day's fighting. The 117th Infantry Regiment replaced us the next morning at about 1030 hours after a cold, sleepless night."

CHAPTER 12

The Battle for Thirimont

On 13 January 1945, the 2nd Battalion of the 120th Infantry Regiment (commanded by Col. Branner P. Purdue) of the 30th Infantry Division was ordered to take Thirimont. The attack started at 0800 hours on 13 January with the support of the American 743rd Tank Battalion and 823rd Tank Destroyer Battalion. The strategy of the operation was a double strike, one from both flanks of the regimental zone aimed at the Germans' probable strongpoints.

Oberschütze Rudi Frühbeisser of *Fallschirmjäger-Regiment 9* describes what happened: "On 13 January at 0600 hours, the troopers were awakened from their sleep in the cellar. A barrage, seemingly like a single impact, came down on Thirimont. The fire increased in volume, and by 0700, it had reached the level of a drumfire barrage. Requests to the staffs of the 2nd and 3rd Battalions were made, but the telephone connections broke after a short while. Sending out signalers to find and fix the break would be murder! Without any orders the paratroopers in the town prepared themselves. What ammunition and hand grenades that were available were shoved into the pockets of the jump suits. We certainly had to prepare for a 'poor man's war' once more! One by one, the squads left the cellars of the houses and took up positions at safe corners to protect themselves from shrapnel."

The 2nd Battalion attacked south to seize Thirimont. In the advance, two German strongpoints were bypassed and had not been reduced at the end of the day's fighting. Mortar and artillery fire were particularly heavy in the area of F Company and only G Company reached the town. Thirimont and the hill (Haute Sarts) were considered by the Germans to be the key to the area, and they clung to them tenaciously. Artillery, mortar, and small arms were deluged upon the attackers.

Frühbeisser continues: "As soon as the fire died down, the troopers walked to their positions reinforcing the other night positions. At 0730 hours, somebody stumbled down the staircase of the cellar to the command post of the 1st Company. It was the company runner, Lance-corporal Franz Hess, an old sweat from the Normandy campaign. Completely out of breath he sat down on the steps of the cellar and told the company commander, *Oberleutnant* Strasser, '*Leutnant,* the Americans have penetrated the town with a regiment of Negroes, prepare a counterattack to be launched immediately!' One man joked that at least Negroes can be spotted easily in the snow!'

"During a short pause in the fire, some squads moved out to reach the prepared trenches and machine gun positions. When they walked through the garden behind the first aid post, a shell hit the depot of the 15th Pioneer Company. The shell penetrated the roof and exploded in the cellar. *Stabsfeldwebel* Schulze, *Obergefreiter* Goldmann, *Obergefreiter* Howe, and *Obergefreiter* Schüssler were killed on the spot. *Obergefreiter* Niehaus and two other men were severely wounded."

How did the Americans manage to get into the western part of Thirimont without getting noticed by the German paratroopers? At the 3rd Company of the 1st Battalion, *Fallschirmjäger-Regiment 9,* which had taken up positions at the northwestern edge of the town, two young soldiers were on sentry duty far out in front of the town. At this post in the dawn, several columns of Americans marched past, one after another. Not being stopped by the sentries there (assumed to be their own troops), the Americans bypassed the 2nd and 3rd Companies, and without running into resistance, the Americans took up positions opposite the church and in another two houses in the southwestern part of the town.

When the 1st Company occupied the houses and took up positions at the windows behind mattresses, they could clearly hear the slow bark of American machine guns between the shell bursts. They could also see several bursts of "exploding peas," as the bright red salvoes of tracer were called, whiz through the town. In the houses everyone took up a 360-degree defense. The objective of the 1st Company was to gain the house across the street, in which there was a bakery.

Leonhardt Maniura of the 15th Pioneer Company of *Fallschirmjäger-Regiment 9* writes: "In the meantime, we had changed quarters once more and were billeted in a house in Ondenval to the left of the main street, nearly the last house in the direction of Thirimont. On 13 January—a Saturday—the Americans increased the mortar fire and German tracked vehicles drove through Ondenval to Thirimont. The Americans had launched a major attack in Thirimont. We, in Ondenval, prepared ourselves in a frantic hurry, were each issued a *Panzerfaust*, apart from our other pack, and were exhorted to leave the troublesome gas masks in the fighting position. We engineers then marched over snow-covered forest and meadow tracks past Vieux Mühle to the edge of Thirimont. Along the way, I wanted to take off my lined camouflage trousers, as they were very obstructive for a quick advance, but did not take them off.

"Above Thirimont, we reached a road, also covered with snow. All of us worked our way forward, crawling closely behind one another. I did not notice that the warhead of my Panzerfaust had broken off and lost, therefore it was useless. Immediately I remembered that the detonator for the hand grenades had remained in the gas mask container in Ondenval! My armament now was: a carbine 98 K with 100 rounds of ammunition and my little pistol (6.35) with four rounds.

"On this snowy road, we really were plastered with shells. Apparently, we made a clear target—later, I learned that an American observer had been located in the church tower at Thirimont. Despite the shelling I kept my gallows humor, because when a shell impacted between me and the crawling squad leader, he shouted, 'Maniura, are both my feet still connected to my body?' I answered, 'Yes, but is my head still attached to my body?' Both of us laughed in relief.

"From this point onward, we had to move down a slight slope to Thirimont. Here crawling soldiers who had gone before had formed a track for us in the snow. I determined that, because a killed *Fallschirmjäger* had been rolled to one side out of this track, we could quickly reach the first house by sliding down, all under an intensive barrage. Having the paratrooper cartridge belts now became a handicap. They were made of cloth, were worn round the neck and attached to the belt. The individual cartridge pouches were closed by snaps. In the crawling and the sliding, I didn't notice that some of the snaps became undone, and I lost part of my ammunition.

"As mentioned, our objective was the first house in Thirimont, coming down this road; my objective was the bog, which was located separately from the house in the courtyard. While my comrades walked into the house—taking cover—I 'assaulted' the bog! I really was not disturbed that the toilet was shaking a bit due to the many shell impacts. For me it simply was a great relief! But only now the danger of my situation became clear to me. I lost no time in pulling up my pants, and jumping, I reached the protective house where I was able to pull them up quietly."

The 2nd Battalion (Lt. Col. James W. Cantey) of the 120th Infantry Regiment opened the attack on the 1st Battalion of *Fallschirmjäger-Regiment 9*—likely under platoon strength—and especially on the 14th Antitank and 15th Pioneer Companies. In reserve were A and C Companies of the 743rd Tank Battalion. The 120th Infantry Regiment's G Company, under the command of Lt. Charles W. Moncrieff, pushed forward with supreme effort and gained the outskirts of Thirimont.

At 0845 hours, G Company was meeting heavy resistance from east and south of Thirimont. The German unit contacted here was the 1st Battalion of *Fallschirmjäger-Regiment 9*. The advance of E and F Companies was stopped by heavy enemy fire. G Company alone continued to advance and fought to the main street in the rural settlement.

At 1145 hours, an infantry counterattack against G Company in the town was contained without loss of ground. Meanwhile, dug-in German troops on the high ground (Haute Sarts) southwest of Thirimont were bringing fire to bear on the troops in town. F Company had been assigned to clear the

Modern view of the road taken by paratroopers of the 15th Company of *Fallschirmjäger-Regiment 9.* HANS WIJERS

route for armor, since the path with G Company guided upon was unsuitable for tanks. But F Company, led by Capt. John M. Jacobsen, met the most petrifying fire, and was forced to halt when the casualty toll reached a demoralizing total. Tanks of the 743rd Tank Battalion endeavoring to break the way hit mines.

The U.S. 743rd Tank Battalion moves toward Thirimont. A Sherman tank with a snow-plough device clears the road.

U.S. ARMY

Leonhardt Maniura resumes his account: "Now the street fighting from house to house began in Thirimont, houses the Americans had not already taken in their big attack. We also took prisoners. Concerns that something could happen, or even fears, did not arise with me; whether one was too 'occupied'? Nearly simultaneously we heard a German MG42 with its typical rapid rate of fire from another house. Joyfully we jumped towards this house and found out too late that the MG42 was manned by Americans. The comrade with the cigarettes was shot in the belly, held his hands in front of his stomach and called for the medic. I do not know whether the medic or the doctor who came up in a hurry managed to help my comrade, as the house-to-house fighting continued."

Unteroffizier Ernst Schumacher, also from the 15th Pioneer Company remembers: "We received orders to attack Thirimont. The town was now taken by the Americans, and we as pioneer company should retake it. After the first attempt to retake the town, our company was heavy beaten, and from its

A drawing of the house-to-house fighting in Thirimont. F. RIESER

150 men strength, only 30 were still alive, this all happened in just one night! Together with my friend Goldmann, we had taken up positions at town entry behind a thick tree, but we were unable to move because American sharpshooters had found our position."

"We were there from 1100 hours until about 1500 hours, under small-arms fire and heavy American artillery fire that poured down on us all the time. We were waiting for the reinforcements of our tanks that should help us to retake Thirimont. Shortly before 1500 hours, we got a nearby hit from the American artillery. Goldmann was hit by shrapnel—one went into the main artery and killed him on the spot."

"At that moment the tank unit [*Kampfgruppe Schenk*, with *Sturmgeschütze* and *Sturmpanzer*] arrived. I moved behind one of the tanks into town. When we reached the centre of town we received heavy artillery fire. I jumped in one of the houses and in the cellar I found back the rest of my company."

Concerned about those mines, Sgt. Perry "Cock" Kelly of the 743rd Tank Battalion stood in the turret of his Sherman tank and swore again at his driver to keep the tank, crawling along in low gear, in the mine-free ruts made in the snow by the passage of previous vehicles. Any slight incline or uneven surface sent the tank slipping sideways. A *thunk* on the outside of the hull brought swearing from Cock as he turned his head and was momentarily stunned by the unexpected appearance of a soldier with snow frozen in his hair. The tank tracks had passed over the feet of the hidden figure. The weight of the tank jerked the dead soldier from underneath his snowy shroud and now rudely held him in a position of attention. The dead were less numerous than mines, but of equal concern in the U.S. zone that had been overrun at the outset of the German offensive the month before. Over two days (13–15 January), the 743rd Tank Battalion lost fifteen tanks to mines.

At that moment, G Company was in possession of a third of Thirimont, but without any support. It had taken about fifty prisoners, but its casualties were also numerous. At 1430 hours, a group of about one hundred German paratroopers was advancing toward the town from the east and was brought under artillery fire and driven off. Late in the day, six assault guns (*Sturmpanzer-Abteilung 217* and *Heeres-Sturmgeschütz-Brigade 98*), two companies of the 3rd Battalion (under *Hauptmann* Rudolf Buchholz) coming from Ondenval, and the 1st Company of *Fallschirmjäger-Regiment 9*, succeeded in entering the town from the east. In an effort to hold the town, American troops retreated to the cellars while American artillery fired POZIT ammunition. However, the artillery fire was ineffective against the German assault guns, and the protection of the houses was available to the German paratroopers as well as the US soldiers.

Lieutenant Robert S. Warnick of G Company, 120th Infantry Regiment, 30th Infantry Division, describes the scene: "We saw soldiers in white camouflage suits coming down the road which our F Company was to take to reinforce us. We shouted toward them, relieved that we finally were receiving some reinforcements. But then the men in the white camouflage suits opened fire on us, and through my binoculars I could make out they were 'Jerry' uniforms. Now we had to huddle up more and continue fighting.

Oskar Klein of *Sturmpanzer-Abteilung 217.*

OSKAR KLEIN / HANS WIJERS

"When we took some prisoners and prepared to send them to the rear, it became clear that we had been encircled. The 'Krauts' also had encircled us from the rear and we realized that we had been cut off in the 'godforsaken village.' Our men fought in every house, in every cellar and from house to house, room to room. We could only hope that E Company soon would break through to us.

"Shortly before noon, we saw a group of about 100 German soldiers attack toward us, and we radioed our artillery to give us all they had! We fought until it became dark, but ammunition got scarce and still we had not received any reinforcements. When we saw even more soldiers come in our direction with tanks, we pulled our 1st platoon forward in order to try to beat off this attack. About this time we received permission to pull back, and our company commander, Lieutenant Moncrieff, assembled his officers to decide how we could pull out of this 'hornet's nest' without too many losses. It was a sticky situation.

"The officers met in a house close to the main road in the village, and it was not an easy thing to get there, as the 'Krauts' covered the road with machine gun fire and everyone who tried to cross the road got a salvo from the MG. We all were discussing how best to get out of here when an enemy tank broke through our lines and cut our company in two.

"The tanks came driving up the road firing directly toward the house where we were. We called up artillery support to keep these tanks away from us but without result, and the tanks fired incessantly at our house and the surrounding houses.

"Nearly half of our company was on the other side of the road. It was stupid trying to reach them, since the road was controlled by the Germans, and we had no means to combat the tank in front of our house. We decided that the men on the other side of the road had to get out of this by themselves. So we tried to get out and most managed to reach the battalion, although Lieutenant Moncrieff was wounded".

Throughout the day on 13 January, attempts were made by the 2nd Battalion, 120th Infantry Regiment, to reinforce Moncrieff's position. F Company could not get by the enemy's roadblock and outpost positions. An attempt was made by 1st Lt. Walter A. Wert Jr. to push E Company through the woods and around the right of F Company to Thirimont. The woods were almost impenetrable, and German troops in dugout positions effectively halted small groups from infiltrating.

The fighting in Thirimont continued throughout the day, and G Company's casualties were mounting. In a telephone conversation made at 1215 hours on 13 January to the corps commander, General Hobbs said: "I had come under the assumption that the big unit (1st Infantry Division) on our left would do something to relieve the pressure on our left. If anything can be done to have some elements on the left push along and take the pressure off, it is essential."

At the end of the day's fighting, elements of G Company were forced to withdraw from Thirimont. The rest of G

Leland S. Hobbs. U.S. ARMY

Company left in Thirimont was later learned to have been captured.

At about 2200 hours, Moncrieff called back to battalion requesting permission to withdraw from the city with the men that remained. Permission was granted and Moncrieff led his company back through the woods along snow covered trails and in inky blackness. Approximately 40 officers and enlisted men returned, of the force of about 110 that had moved out with G Company that morning. The strength of G Company on 13 January 1945 was 163 enlisted men and 5 officers. On 14 January, it was 84 enlisted men and 3 officers.

In the meantime, it had become dark, but the area was brightly lit by the partially burning houses in Thirimont. From time to time, shots were fired, but the battle for Thirimont was over for now. The 4th Company of *Fallschirmjäger-Regiment 9* suffered the highest losses in the fight for Thirimont: 21 killed and 12 wounded.

General Hobbs was at the battalion command post and spoke with Lieutenant Moncrieff before he was evacuated. Plans were meanwhile being completed for an attack on

Thirimont by the 1st Battalion, and the remnants of G Company were assigned to help F Company take a strongpoint outside the town at the same time. The strongpoint was a tough
objective, particularly for so battered a company as F Company, and it was not seized until after the fall of Thirimont.

At about midnight, the 2nd Battalion of the 120th Infantry
Regiment, had withdrawn to their position occupied before
the morning attack had been launched. Meanwhile, after supporting the initial attack by fire, the 1st Battalion, 120th
Infantry Regiment, 30th Infantry Division, was in readiness for
an attack on Ligneuville and had moved forward toward
Baugnez.

CHAPTER 13

Situation of the 30th Infantry Division

The U.S. 30th Infantry Division continued its attack to the south, advanced approximately 3,000 yards against moderate resistance across rough terrain covered with snow, seized the towns of Ligneuville, Hedomont, Lamonriville, Reculemont, Thioux, Villers, and Bellevaux, and in a night attack reached the outskirts of Thirimont. The division seized the high ground and established bridgeheads across the Amel River south of the towns of Ligneuville and Bellevaux.

During the night of 13–14 January, a patrol from the 119th Infantry Regiment reached the town of Thioux and reported it unoccupied. The same patrol heard movement of vehicles and talking in the town of Bellevaux.

Staff officer *Oberstleutnant i.G.* Dietrich Moll of the *18th Volksgrenadier-Division* noted in a report written after the war: "On 13 January 1945, the expected enemy attack began. Strong enemy forces from Malmédy attacked in the direction of Ligneuville. Tanks supported by heavy artillery fire pushed our brave men from *Grenadier-Regiment 293* back to a line going from Baugnez to Bellevaux.

"The next day, the enemy broke through our defense line into Ligneuville. The town was already prepared for to be destroyed, but because of the chaos, it fell before we had a change to destroy it, in enemy hands. Enemy tanks arrived at the south end of the River Amblève, but were pushed back by our tank destroyer unit before they could cross the river.

"The Pioneer Battalion received orders to block the road Pont–Recht and to destroy all crossroads. At the same time,

Soldiers of the U.S. 119th Infantry Regiment enter Ligneuville.
U.S. ARMY

the bridges of the railroad line Born–Recht–Petit Thier were prepared for demolition.

"Also on the left flank, the enemy attacked with strong units. To cover the gap on the right side, *Grenadier-Regiment*

Modern view of the road leading to the hilltop, Haute Sarts.

HANS WIJERS

294 was ordered to pull back on a line from Ochsenbaracke (north of Kaiserbaracke)–Poteau–Petit-Thier."

"The Artillery Regiment was placed in new positions in the area of Born–Wieschen (one kilometer southwest of Recht)–Nieder-Emmelser Heide."

"On 15 January 1945, enemy infantry and tanks crossed the River Emmels and pushed back *Grenadier-Regiment 293* to the ridge of a forest south of Ligneuville and Pont. After our tank destroyer unit knocked out many tanks, they had many casualties themselves and lost most of their own guns."

The weakened *18th Volksgrenadier Division* was completely surprised when they received a replacement battalion of 500 men who were assigned to the division and divided amongst the grenadier regiments. The division's headquarters was moved on the southwestern edge of Born.

Farther northwest in the *3rd Fallschirmjäger-Division*'s area, after an attack, the U.S. 30th Infantry Division reached the outskirts of Thirimont. A patrol from the 3rd Battalion of the

120th Infantry Regiment moved toward Hill 551 (Haute Sarts), southwest of Thirimont in an effort to secure the heights and protect their troops in the town from the south. However, the fire of German paratroopers who were entrenched on the top of the hill with automatic weapons drove the patrol back.

CHAPTER 14

The Second Attack on Thirimont

At 0030 hours on 14 January, the 1st Battalion of the 120th Infantry Regiment, under Lt. Col. Ellis W. Williamson, attacked through the badly mauled 2nd Battalion for the objective of Thirimont. The battalion encountered extreme difficulty in attempting to move through the blackness of the night, the woods, and the falling snow. At almost 0600 hours, the battalion had advanced through the enemy outposts on the outskirts of Thirimont. The temperature was dropping steadily, and a further difficulty was encountered with radio communication. The cold caused the radios to malfunction in many cases, and radio control of the units became difficult. Coupled with the fact that enemy artillery still rained down from German positions in the vicinity of Ondenval, very little progress was made against Thirimont.

At the same time, an advance party from B Company, 1st Battalion, moved out from "Five Points" to establish a block on the Ligneuville road, 1,000 yards east of the high ground at Huyer.

The remainder of the battalion followed when the road-block was set up, moved 1000 yards south almost to the block, then swung east into the Pange Stream valley and up the steep banks and winding road into Thirimont. The riflemen of C Company led the way. That company was to seize the rear out-skirts of the town; then A and B Companies were to push through and take the remainder of Thirimont.

Captain Pulver, commander of B Company, 1st Battalion, 120th Infantry Regiment, 30th Infantry Division, remembers:

"On the evening of 13 January, our company was given orders to attack along the Ligneuville road to set up a roadblock to prevent the approach of enemy armored vehicles. The 3rd Platoon was issued rubber boots for wading the Amblève River. They were then to take up defensive positions to guard the area while the engineers were building a foot bridge. But late in the evening orders were changed and we were redirected southeast toward Thirimont to assist the 2nd Battalion.

"Sgt. Wally Miller was leading the way. He was about to open the door of a house near the road, when the door was opened for him by a German soldier coming out. Without hesitation, Sergeant Miller snapped a quick shot killing the German. A hail of bullets ensued from within the house. In his haste to get away, SgtMiller lost his rifle and helmet as well as the skull cap he had worn since those distant days on the Vire Canal in Normandy.

"While we continued forward on the road, C Company surrounded the house and took several prisoners. We reached the outskirts of Thirimont just at daybreak."

There was a deep snow, which hampered the advance of the unit's tanks and tank destroyers alike. Thirimont and the heights to the south of it were deemed difficult to take by the Americans, and they saw it as a difficult job.

At 0445 hours German artillery, mortars, snipers, and light machine guns fired on the Americans, and resistance increased steadily until in the early dawn, the battalion was forced to halt.

Captain Pulver continues: "C Company moved to our left but was immediately pinned down in a gully just short of a row of houses. Our company began receiving heavy machine gun fire from Hill 551 on our right. Since we were unable to move from our exposed position, I sent Sgt. Henderson and his squad around our right flank with the mission of knocking out the machine gun that was giving us so much trouble. We were learning that every house in the village was a bastion. The thick stone walls of the homes made excellent supporting forts, with rifles and automatic weapons firing from every window and opening. Sergeant Henderson's squad met with disaster—three killed and the rest captured. The Germans actually marched these prisoners down the hill to the village in plain view, and we could do nothing to save them."

Snow hampered any armored support; tanks bogged down in the soft stream bottom. Patrols sent to flank German strong points were unable to advance. When daylight began to glimmer over the housetops, it became suicidal to attempt to move heavy weapons over the open ground to support the battalion, and the plans for A and B Companies to go though C Company were postponed. C Company pushed slowly onto its outskirts objective and held its ground along the hedgerows which zigzagged on either side of the road. At 1330 hours came a light counterattack in which thirty paratroopers and an assault gun were repelled.

Fritz Roppelt, a forward observer in the 12th Company of *Fallschirmjäger-Regiment 9*, describes the situation: "Via radio, I informed the battalion and regimental command posts that the Americans in Thirimont noiselessly had advanced to the main road from Calvary to Church! Mired in thoughts and watching for shell holes in the foggy snow, we came to Calvary. Near the top of the first house we noticed a spy hole, and it took only one look for me to grasp the entire situation: as far as one could see down the main road at Thirimont there were Yanks standing around, and in front of them, with raised hands, were captured members of 2nd Company, *Fallschirmjäger-Regiment 9*. Once more, they had not heeded my warnings not to take up combat positions in the houses, but 100 meters to the north of it!"

Inside Thirimont, elements of *Fallschirmjäger-Regiment 9* had set up an iron-clad defense, and they fought with great tenacity. As darkness was closing in, about 1730 hours, German paratroopers of the 1st Battalion counterattacked with one battalion of infantry advancing in waves and supported by one company of *Sturmpanzer* and assault guns.

Oberschütze Rudi Frühbeisser of *Fallschirmjäger-Regiment 9* recalls: "At dawn on 14 January, *Oberleutnant* Strasser was ordered by battalion commander, *Hauptmann* Schiffke, to clear the town of Americans that have penetrated it with an energetic counterattack. The partially burning houses gave off enough light for this."

C Company, 1st Battalion, 120th Infantry Regiment in the lead rallied its fire power, and called for artillery. The Germans pushed furiously forward to within fifty yards of the hastily dug in lines of C Company along the hedgerows and roadways making Thirimont a complicated network. There two assault guns were knocked out by artillery fire, but the paratroopers still advanced.

The paratroopers managed to retake the center of the village and chase out the American troops. They ran into smaller groups, which often had set up road blocks with only three men and waited for relief. Large amounts of booty were taken. For the Americans, partially captured in the cellars and partially in the counterattack, the fight was over. In the village there were many dead Americans.

Frühbeisser continues: "*Oberleutnant* Strasser returned to the command post and reported to his commander, *Hauptmann* Schiffke: 'Order executed, town cleared of enemy, 92 captured Americans and large amounts of booty. Our losses are slight!' Ammunition and hand grenades were distributed; captured weapons and supplies also were used. Some anti-tanks guns and mortars also were captured. These weapons were positioned in the village and prepared for action.

"In the afternoon a heavy barrage again came down on the damaged town. At dusk the Americans attacked the town from the road toward Sedan and the hamlet of Grosbois, but were partially blocked by an immediate counterattack. Apart from harassing fire, the night remained quiet."

In the meantime, the positions of the 3rd Battalion, 120th Infantry Regiment, 30th Infantry Division, on Huyer were taken over by the 117th Infantry Regiment at 1030 hours on 14 January. (L Company of the 3rd Battalion was attached to the 117th Infantry Regiment until 1600 hours, when it reverted to battalion control.)

Destroyed assault guns near Thirimont, most likely the ones put out of action on 14 January.

Alan D. McGraw, a squad leader in I Company, 3rd Battalion, 120th Infantry Regiment, 30th Infantry Division, recollects: "After leaving Malmédy, our unit was assigned a hill ('Huyer') on the south of the town. The squad area we replaced had been manned by nineteen men. We covered it with five. We had several patrols and an occasional attack here and there, but always returning to Malmédy."

Pine covered and even higher than Huyer, Haute Sarts (Hill 551) was known to be full of German snipers who had caused numerous casualties among the U.S. troops in Thirimont. It presented a formidable problem, but it was the principle key to the entire Ligneuville sector. At 1150 hours, 3rd Battalion crossed the line of departure and moved generally parallel to the road from Baugnez, striking Haute Sarts from the northwest. Along the road where destroyed American vehicles were still lying in testimony of the German breakthrough, men met constant harassment by artillery and rocket shells, aimed at the obvious route of advance.

Tech Sergeant A. P. Wiley of the 2nd Platoon, M Company, 120th Infantry Regiment, writes: "We then moved around Hill 541 on the road to Haute Sarts and jumped off about noon. We were in thick woods and under constant small arms fire, but we continued to move past Haut Sarts and turned to attack Thirimont from the northwest. The 2nd Battalion of the 120th Infantry Regiment had attempted to capture Thirimont the day before, but they had been turned back in a fierce fight that resulted in many casualties in the 2nd Battalion. We were about to find out what the 2nd Battalion had been through and that Thirimont was the key defensive position for the Germans."

Into the draw of the Pange Stream the troops ran across the open ground up the hill toward the heights ahead. The Germans were prepared. They had chosen positions for their automatic fire and artillery observation posts which were impossible to detect.

Alan D. McGraw continues: "Then on 14 January, we were to take Hill 551. On the way our commander, Lieutenant Andrews, was killed and shortly after that my BAR man, Ed Belicek, was shot in his left arm. The bullet entered above his left wrist and traveled up his arm and exited out his shoulder. There was a little stream right before the approach to the hill. Some tanks had been running around there before we got there. Although the ice had began to refreeze, I and others went through up to our waists. The snow was knee deep."

Leading the 3rd Battalion in what was to become an historic battle was I Company, still so sorely in need of replacements that it functioned as a platoon. Behind was to follow K Company. The lead company gained the second hedgerow on Hill 551 before receiving any opposition.

With the mission of seizing the hill, alone if necessary, and then to give supporting fire to the 1st Battalion in Thirimont, I Company swung right (south) and then headed up the hill (northeast), in an effort to strike the enemy from the rear.

Alan D. McGraw again: "As we got nearly three-quarters the way up the hill, we ran into a larger German force coming down. After the initial fire and shooting slowed down, we managed to get some fox holes started."

All at once, then, when I Company was 250 yards from the top of the hill, the Germans, who had gained positions by that time, began to fight back with terrifying intensity. The German superiority in numbers soon began to tell, for though I Company struggled bravely on, it could not prevent the Germans from gradually encircling it; almost a battalion was combating a mere platoon.

McGraw continues: "After lying in the snow all the rest of the day, waiting for support or relief, I was wet from the waist down, and I was sure I was going to freeze to death, so I asked Lt. John Doyle, our platoon leader, if I could go back and try to find some dry clothes. I felt bad about leaving because we only had fourteen men left in the whole company. As I approached the aid station a truck stopped and a bunch of guys got off, they threw off a bunch of overcoats, and I grabbed one. It had six packs of Camel cigarettes in one of the pockets. Anyway, the doctors cut my boots off my feet which were a light shade of blue. I told him if I could get some dry clothes, I was going back up. He tied a tag on my big toe and said, 'Son, you're going to the hospital.' I'll never forget that day as long as I live."

Francis W. Curry.

I Company men kept hoping K Company would appear to help in the assault. A runner sent to contact K Company returned to find that in the meantime I Company had been forced to withdraw and leave about a half squad, which had been cut off, either captured or killed. K Company was struggling, too. In and around one house, the Germans had set up a pillbox, and as K Company advanced over the snow, in the open, the Germans let go with their maximum.

Squad leader Sgt. Francis W. Curry, who had distinguished himself a month before at the paper mill near Malmédy, observed where the strongpoint was, and with two of his pals ran 200 yards toward the house. The three men ducked into a barn next door for cover. The buddies all came from upstate New York, and they fought with an ardent and unbeatable teamwork. With rifles and hand grenades, they fought the Germans on the ground floor of the house, forcing them at last to go upstairs. Private First Class Raymond W. Gould had distinguished himself by leading a squad to knock out a strong-point on Huyer; now he ran to a back window to catch the Germans by surprise. As he climbed in, however, a German observation post nearby saw him and cut him down. Sergeant Francis W. Curry and his other comrade, PFC Adam Lucero, did not hesitate a moment; they fired a BAR and threw hand grenades into the upstairs from outside until they were fired on from another enemy position. They went inside and fired through the windows; soon they had forced the enemy upstairs again. The remainder of the squad had come to the barn, meanwhile, and was firing persistently through the walls and windows of the house. For three and a half hours the scrap continued.

At 1730 hours, Sergeant Curry had his men put hay in the house from the barn and ignite it. Soon the house was aflame, and the Germans were forced to withdraw, with losses, into the night. The pillbox was reduced, and the two pals responsible were unscathed.

There were many better-installed strongpoints, however, and though I and K Companies finally gained contact, darkness found the 3rd Battalion digging in 500 yards short of their objective. Patrols were sent out to reconnoiter the areas to the flanks.

At dawn on 15 January, another heavy barrage came down on Thirimont and the surrounding hamlets. This time the Americans used only phosphorous shells. The effect was destructive. The entire day there was fierce defensive fighting in Thirimont and vicinity against the advancing Americans. From dawn, things were very intense for the 2nd and 3rd Battalions of *Fallschirmjäger-Regiment 9*. At the regimental command post, located at the monastery of Montenau, reports came in one after another. Here also at dawn a murderous artillery barrage began. Soon the individual telephone wires were broken and the use of runners was replaced by radio communication.

On 15 January, the battalions resumed the attack with a superhuman effort. Just before dawn, the Germans directed a two-company attack against the 1st Battalion clinging to the outskirts of Thirimont. Two hours later, at 0815 hours, Lt. Col. Ellis W. Williamson, 1st Battalion commander, sent A Company on the left and B Company on the right to strike the remainder of the town. The Germans called their utmost support and threw all their strength against the attackers. The Germans were in an unusually advantageous position to do so. Indeed, the whole town was a bastion, a defense town of ideal specifications. Its approximately 100 houses were for the most part thick walled, stone farmhouses, spaced at distances of from 50 to 100 yards. Edging forward, the riflemen faced a series of bristling forts, irregularly spaced pillboxes, from whose windows automatic weapons were mutually protecting. Wherever they could, the German troops utilized the cellars, and, considering themselves invulnerable, they flayed the advance with persistent fire. Later men were to say, 'the sniper fire both from the houses and the hill Haute Sarts was terrifying.

Captain Pulver, commander of B Company, 1st Battalion, 120th Infantry Regiment, writes: "Colonel Williamson informed me via 300 radio that the commander of A Company had been killed and asked if I could spare Lieutenant Hunn. Lieutenant Minyard had left a few days before Christmas, but the three sergeants, Maybee, Johnson, and Barnett, had just returned to the company the day after New Year's, and I still had Lieutenant LePage. A Company had been very unfortunate in losing three commanders. Lieutenant Hunn commented, as he bid me so long, 'Will I be next?'"

Men who walked upright for only a second or two would drop dead. None could trace where the shot came from. There was Captain Pulver (commanding officer of B Company), who walked around as straight as a flagpole, directing tanks and leading them into positions; how he escaped being killed is a mystery. Anybody else who stood up for long dropped again for a lot longer.

The solution to the pillbox fighting soon appeared to be the use of tanks' and tank destroyers' primary weapons. The tracked vehicles moved to positions behind the hedgerows or houses and blasted at the pillboxes causing the most difficulty. The tankers fired on the basements for several minutes; then infantry troops rushed at the house and reduced it. In all cases, it was slow going; it was hard persuading the Germans that after their victory drive toward the Meuse and Liege, they were actually going to be pushed back into Germany again.

Captain Pulver again: "The colonel called me again to tell me that there were six tank destroyers on the road behind us and that, if I could find a way to get them forward, they would help out. Did we need help! Somehow I got back to them and guided them forward across a stream and up a steep hill. It was slippery going, but they finally groaned their way to the front.

"I got two of the tank destroyers to fire on a large complex that was giving us a bad time. This consisted of a stone house, with connected barn. After about ten rounds from the cannons of the tank destroyers, a white flag was seen waving from an upstairs window. I moved Sergeant Dale's squad forward to receive the surrender. Forty white-suited German paratroopers filed out the door with their hands up. We lined them up on the road in front of the house preparatory to moving them to the rear when an enemy machine gun up the hill on our right fired into their ranks killing five and wounding two of their own men as well as two of ours. We quickly dove into a ditch. The commander of one of our tank destroyers saw the whole thing and blasted the German machine-gun position.

"Our prisoners suddenly became very friendly. One who could speak English volunteered to help evacuate their own as well as our wounded. Doors were ripped off their hinges to serve as litters and the whole column was soon on its way to medical vehicles about a mile away."

One of the German paratroopers that were among the prisoners, and helping carry out the wounded American soldiers, was Leonhardt Maniura of the 15th Pioneer Company of *Fallschirmjäger-Regiment 9:* "At dusk I entered a house with my carbine at the ready, and for the first time saw civilians in Thirimont (in Amel and Ondenval very few civilians had been seen). They were treating a severely wounded American soldier which was on a stretcher. Next to him was a tasty looking evening meal: we saw all this by candle light since there was no electricity. In a way I felt sorry for the wounded man, but I really pitied the civilian population, for they had been pulled into this fight without bearing any guilt for it. The civilians asked me not to do anything to the American. That was not my intention at all! I continued looking round the house to see whether any Americans were lurking in there, and then continued without having been offered anything to eat. But I really would have had no time for that, and I was not really hungry anyway.

"Near the edge of Thirimont, we entered a farm building that was encircled by a wall. It slowly was getting dark. A while later other soldiers, like us in white camouflage clothing, entered the building through the open door. We looked at each other, very distrusting and hostile, and for the first time I had a scary feeling, as there was no possibility of cover in the enclosed courtyard and we were a smaller group. Thank God it soon became clear that they also were German soldiers. We knew from experience that two groups of enemy soldiers could walk next to each other on a street without recognizing each other until somebody spoke up and then they learned they were enemies! The *Fallschirmjäger* helmets without a rim around the edge also looked more like American helmets than normal German ones.

"We continued in the dark past the edge of Thirimont to an isolated farm where we entrenched in a shed built next to the house. We defended the farm until the next day until our ammunition was used up. I helped our ensign by recharging the magazines of his submachine gun, as he only had two magazines but a ration bag full of ammo. We formed a small combat group, fewer than twenty soldiers at this farm, and if I'm not mistaken, an officer was also present. The many bullets striking the tin wall of the shed made a very terrible noise, but the wall absorbed the bullets.

"In the meantime, we became encircled by the Americans. No withdrawal toward the town was possible after the ammunition ran out. By 0900 on 14 January 1945—Sunday—we held a

Modern views of the farm opposite the church in Thirimont
where U.S. soldiers took up positions. HANS WIJERS

white flag out of a window and indeed, no further shots came
from the Americans. We put down our weapons in the rather
large shed. In doing so I hid my pistol in a drawer hoping I
might be able to collect is soon."

Thirimont is captured. U.S. soldiers have parked their jeep next to one of the destroyed buildings. U.S. ARMY

Lieutenant John D'Amico reported by 1330 hours that A Company, 1st Battalion, 120th Infantry Regiment, had taken its objective and consolidated its defense. Only a few minutes before the attack the former executive officer had taken over A Company. The old company commander, Lt. Edward W. Hunn, had suffered what he thought was superficial wound, a scratch on his back; he had fought steadily on until a few moments before the jump-off for the final objective, the eastern outskirts of the town. Then, suddenly he collapsed; it was later found that the bullet had pierced the small of his back, ricocheted off his small rib and had rammed itself into his chest just below the heart. The bullet was found to be wooden, a device which the Germans were remembered to use during the desperate close combat fighting of the hedgerows in Normandy. Tired, but sticking to their dug in outposts on the edge of the town, the men of Lieutenant D' Amico's A Company knew the enemy had been desperate and fanatical. But not strong enough.

Infantrymen of the 30th Division carry a wounded German soldier to a battalion aid station in Thirimont.

With the aid of skid chains, an American half-track pulls out of a roadside ditch near Thirimont.

CHAPTER 15

Clearing Hill 551

West of Thirimont, the battle continued to rage. On 15 January, at 0815 hours, the 3rd Battalion, 120th Infantry Battalion, 30th Infantry Division, had attacked again, and in the afternoon, only small, costly progress had been made. Help was requested.

In the command post of the 2nd Battalion, 120th Infantry Battalion, whose E and F Companies had been withdrawn to Waimes from their dug in positions before Thirimont, plans had been made to take the high ground called 'Wolfsbusch', 300 yards south of Thirimont, and across the Amblève (Amel) river. Accordingly, at 1315 hours, E Company, followed by the remainder of the Battalion at 1415 hours, left Waimes by truck, and detrucked at the road junction 800 yards south of Baugnez. The troops then started for their objective on foot.

At 1600 hours, orders came to Lt. Col. James W. Cantey, commanding officer of the 2nd Battalion, to return to help the 3rd Battalion. Colonel Purdue had divided Hill 551 into two areas; the southern portion was to be the 3rd Battalion objective, the north half the 2nd Battalion's.

The 2nd Battalion returned to the initial road junction where it had detrucked, and from a line of departure there, attacked, with G and F Companies in the lead. The 3rd Battalion pushed with renewed effort at the same time. Light tanks could have speeded the taking of the objective, and continues effort was made to get them on the high ground. The steep slope was covered with more than two feet of snow, however, and the tanks bogged down again and again.

Late in the morning, L Company had run into a strong point. A platoon led by T/Sgt. Monte W. Keener was pinned down from a machine gun whose location was impossible to discern. The men tried to move forward; a squad leader jumped up aggressively and ran a few yards, when a sputtering from a hidden gun caused him to fall dead in the snow. Another man had already started forward and had gone about twenty yards when the fire cut him dead too. Before it could be knocked out, so the platoon could advance, Keener knew that the emplacement had to be found. Decisively he jumped up to make a rush; as he ran, he surveyed hastily the terrain, and when the bullets snapped around him, he lunged toward where he thought they had originated. He had gone twenty-five yards when he saw the enemy grouped around the death dealing weapon. He yelled to his men and pointed to the location; then he dropped to his knee and fired his BAR into the nest. His men were moving to knock out the emplacement, when, hit by the machine gun he had discovered Keener fell forward on his face.

Lieutenant William H. Callaway had brought his own platoon up on the right of Keener's. Having seen Keener, and taking in the situation at a glance, he organized his own platoon for a flanking raid on the nest, grabbed what he could of the adjacent platoon, and sweeping around fifty yards right of the German position, he assaulted the emplacement and destroyed it, killing the complete German machine-gun crew and capture five more Germans, defending the position.

Continuing to lead the two platoons, Calloway dispersed his men in a wooded area near the crest of Haute Sarts. Though L Company was trying to move forward, he knew that if his men left their positions, the infiltrating enemy who were sniping at them and the enemy who was delivering the flanking fire pinning down L Company, would gain an advantage and the hill would have to be taken again. He realized that while his men held the ground, someone would have to annihilate the enemy positions.

Still struggling uphill, the tanks were gaining the high ground an open field away from Lieutenant Callaway. Though one man had been killed and another wounded taking the

An American soldier stands next to one of the destroyed assault guns near Thirimont.

exposed short cut, he dashed across a field and down a path to meet the tanks and bring them forward. Up the hill 600 yards to a point close to German strong points he led them. Once the tanks had gained vantage points near the crest of the hill, the Germans were, after a stiff fight, beaten. Lieutenant Callaway used a tank to evacuate nine wounded men of his platoon. He had a full day.

Capt. George R. Reeves of L Company was another hero of the day. He had exposed himself to direct artillery fire on positions which were holding up his company. A sniper sighted him, and he felt a sharp crack at his hip, but on inspection found a bullet had pierced his clothing, his wallet and field glasses without even scratching him.

During this struggle on Hill 551, Capt. "Indian Joe" Reaser of K Company was wounded. His executive officer, Lt. Glyn Persons, took command and distinguished himself conspicuously. Later, he also was wounded, and his executive, in turn, took command.

By night, Hill 551 had fallen into the hands of the American troops. Eighty-seven prisoners of war were taken, although most of the German paratroopers fought ferociously, and many got killed. Three consecutive days of fighting had brought a long casualty for the 120th Infantry Regiment, too. It paused for a day to reorganize and consolidate its gains. Patrols cleared the area south of Haute Sarts to the river.

General Hobbs, the division commander, entered the 3rd Battalion's command post on the day after the fight. He spoke to Colonel Purdue about the bitterness of the battle: "The Germans had outdone themselves in organizing clever, deceptive, powerful defenses on the ground. The Germans had fought viciously for each inch. But the men of the 30th Infantry Division, of the 120th Infantry Regiment, had overcome terrible obstacles. Not easily, no. But with a fortitude and persistence that did honor to every man associated with the unit."

The general complimented Greer. Hill 551 was as hard a battle as was fought in this war, in the Pacific of the European theater. Men agreed on that. Then the general and the colonel left the command post.

CHAPTER 16

The Battle for Faymonville

The U.S. 1st Infantry Division received orders from V Corps headquarters. The division attacked east to seize the approaches of the "Ondenval Defile." This was a stretch of open, gently rolling country which began at Ondenval, northwest of Amblève, and extended southwest to form a natural corridor. The initial objectives for the 1st Infantry Division were Faymonville and Schoppen.

The going was tough. There was a noticeable withdrawal of German forces in several thinly held spots, but still the resistance of the Germans was as stubborn and as pronounced as at the beginning of the drive. The weather continued extremely cold; snow was still piled up four and five feet deep. The sharp, cutting wind whipped the snow into drifts and it continued to snow. Complete mine detection was next to impossible, and in at least one case a tank was knocked out by one of the U.S. mines.

Lance Corporal "Smiling Al" Alvarez of C Company, 16th Infantry Regiment, 1st Infantry Division, remembers: "Rumors were now flying that we would attack Faymonville the first week of January 1945. So we took under fire all possible enemy positions in the town. Methodically, we increased the destruction by dropping high-explosive rounds through the roofs, and then followed up with white phosphorus to burn the houses. Most of them, however, were constructed of stone and resisted all our bombardments. Still, slowly, Faymonville was systematically pulverized. During that first week of January, in conjunction with the mortars, we fired in support of a patrol attempting to retrieve the body of Lieutenant McLaughlin, of L Company, killed days before.

Ruins in Faymonville. J. PFEIFFER

"Lieutenant Cangelosi 'had the word,' and got us ready by checking our equipment, clothing and footwear. 'I want constant commo while on the attack,' he said. 'The infantry is going to get us on high ground every chance they can, and protect us, too.' That's good, but for me, first I must get warm. Layering of clothing was the answer. So it's long underwear, shirts. jackets, many trousers, ponchos, wrapped blanket strips over straw, and joining the 'monster footprint brigade.' With a French Foreign Legion 'kepi' look, I covered my helmet with a white pillow slip with a flap covering my neck. Then I enclosed myself in a white bed sheet, a snow cape, and emerged through the slit for my head. Finally, I connected up the radio and set it on a German wooden sled with a 50-foot on/off switch for the lieutenant's use. We were 'ready for Freddy.'

"Threw some cardboard ammo cartons filled with coffee, sugar and cans of cream on the sled and loaded my pockets with 'goodies.' Now, as the last preparation, I ate everything I could find of rations: crackers, cheese, meat and beans, cocoa, sugar, candy . . . anything for energy. 'Now bring on those Krauts. I'm warm, full and have dry feet. I can shoot, scoot, and communicate.'"

Two Sherman tanks of the 745th Tank Battalion, knocked out by mines. J. PFEIFFER

It was into this weather, in heavy snowdrifts that the 3rd Battalion of the American 16th Infantry Regiment, 1st Infantry Division, commanded by Lt. Col. Charles T. Horner, and with elements (tanks and 1st Battalion of the 16th Infantry Regiment) of Task Group Davisson attacked Faymonville on 15 January.

Oberschütze Walter Wittlinger of the 2nd Battalion staff of *Fallschirmjäger-Regiment 9*: "The Americans were attacking the town of Faymonville with artillery preparation. Captain Harth ordered us runners to enter the fight at the railway underpass. When we orientated ourselves on the spot, no one was there except us. Infantry small arms fire, mortars and artillery was very intense. It was a sign that the Americans have not managed to penetrate very far. We returned to the battalion command post and reported on the situation. Around midday a report came in that the Americans had occupied the command post of the 5th Company. Captain Harth was then seized by ambition and he said, 'Then we'll throw them out again!'

"All available men were committed (*Hauptmann* Harth, *Oberleutnant* Gutermann, the liaison officer, and we runners). With two *Panzerfausts*, one bazooka, carbines, and pistols, we tried to advance in the direction of Waimes under fire. Without any losses we reached the vicinity (about twenty meters) of the command post of 5th Company. The Americans responded with intense rifle fire. To our left an anti-tank gun was positioned in such a way that it could not fire on the house. The liaison (lance corporal) who had the two Panzerfausts prepared one for firing. He took up a firing position and pushed the button. What happened? The *Panzerfaust* flew about ten meters and then fell to the ground without exploding. The same thing happened with the second *Panzerfaust*. Only the bazooka, also fired at the house, reached the target."

Alvarez continues his story: "We (I was pulling the sled with the radio) accompanied I Company, and later L Company. When we slowly approached the northeastern part of Faymonville, some tanks of the 745th Tank Battalion drove onto mines. Our soldiers advanced under heavy fire of enemy

Modern view of the railroad bridge in Faymonville. HANS WIJERS

mortars and machine guns. According to the first reports of losses, in 3rd Battalion two men were killed and fifteen wounded. We stopped at nightfall and ran a line to the nearest company. To hear reports of seventy casualties for the 1st Battalion! We fired harassing missions and kept everyone awake that night."

Hauptmann Elard Harth, commanding the 2nd Battalion of *Fallschirmjäger-Regiment 9* since *Major* Taubert became sick, had his hands full, trying to avoid the worst for his troopers. The afternoon of the counterattack on Faymonville, in which some houses once again were captured, the new battalion commander, Captain Harth, was killed. The adjutant, *Oberleutnant* Willi Gutermann, took over command of the battalion.

The attack of the 3rd Battalion of the U.S. 16th Infantry Regiment (1st Infantry Division) was stopped north of Faymonville. In the war diary of the 16th Infantry Regiment it is reported that the 3rd Battalion got itself stuck in a hornets' nest in a little wood east of Faymonville. Only by a hard and bloody attack by K Company was this little wood cleared of the

Aerial view of Faymonville after heavy bombardment by U.S. artillery.

enemy. Later the 1st Battalion, which was still in reserve behind the front, was able to chase the paratroopers of 2nd Battalion of *Fallschirmjäger-Regiment 9* from the northern part of Faymonville.

Private First Class Harry P. Pritts of A Company, 1st Battalion, 16th Infantry Regiment, 1st Infantry Division, remembers: "17 December 1944, I had my first baptism under fire as I entered the front line. There are many veterans of the Battle of the Bulge, but very few that were left at Faymonville. We had orders to take Faymonville on the morning of 15 January 1945. It was a very cold, crisp morning; temp must have been around forty degrees below zero and thirteen or fourteen inches of snow on the ground.

"My unit, A Company, crossed a small river or canal with water in it to our waist. The water was so swift that it had not frozen. Two hundred feet from the river or canal was the railroad, and it was elevated about nine or ten feet. The Germans had machine guns set up across on the off side tracks which we soon disposed of. Then we went up a small grade of 800 yards to a knoll with a large field of approximately 50 acres. There was a 40 to 50 foot drop in the center of the field with a slope down 400 yards and a slope back up 400 yards to the outskirts of town.

"I was in reserve squad, and by the time I got to the top of the ridge the first of the company was within 100 yards of the hedgerow. That was when the Germans started firing and everyone hit the ground. I found a fence post which I broke off and started to push snow ahead of myself and built a snow fort. I tried to keep the post close to my face. We were to have tank support as we advanced up the railroad, and when the .50 calibers opened fire we thought our tanks were closing in. We found out later that it was machine guns captured in the Bulge, and we were on the wrong end. About an hour after entering the field, seven of us got up and back over the ridge where the tanks were to travel.

"We found the railroad station 200 yards from town and got in it by 0930 hours. We built a fire in the stove as four of us had frozen feet. I then said that we may as well be captured or shot for we would surely freeze to death. Fortunately, none of these things happened. We thawed out and warmed up and counted the bullet holes in our clothing and gear. I had fifteen rounds through my bedroll and two through my jacket sleeve; none had even touched my skin."

War Diary of the F Company, 16th Infantry Regiment reported the following line for 14 and 15 January 1945: "Company awaiting attack orders."

Wittlinger of *Fallschirmjäger-Regiment 9* resumes his account: "From the house a shout went up, 'Don't shoot, our people are here!' Captain Harth rose and went toward the house. A shot, Captain Harth fell to the ground; he did not move. He couldn't be recovered, because firing from the house was very strong. But who shouted? Was it possible that our own men of the 5th Company were in the house or was it a GI?

"*Oberleutnant* Gutermann and the liaison also were wounded. The liaison was wounded in the upper thigh. Both could get back to the first aid post without any help from others. I was on the right embankment of the road behind a small tree, which hardly offered me any protection. In front of me several projectiles hit the ground, but I was lucky and was not hit. We could not spot the sniper. I suspected that the sniper had lifted one of the roof tiles and was firing through the slit. The firing of the bazooka, which torched the house, had created a pause in the firing. We didn't know whether the Americans had withdrawn. Perhaps it was a trap? We waited to see. We did not know whether someone at the gun crew was wounded. We tried to recover *Hauptmann* Harth, but our attempt was fired on. A further attempt was useless, as our armament was (one carbine, plus I had one quick-firing Italian rifle, and there was little ammunition left). Tank noise was heard coming toward us. We tried to get into a house and succeeded where we awaited further developments.

"During a pause in the firing we tried to return to the battalion command post and reached it without any difficulty. We reported to *Leutnant* Lewin (during our absence he remained in the command post), '*Hauptmann* Harth fallen, First Lieutenant Gutermann and the liaison wounded, two runners returned from the command post of 5th Company. *Hauptmann* Harth could not be recovered, despite two attempts. *Oberleutnant* Gutermann and the liaison could get back to the first aid post without any help.'

"We remained in the battalion command post. In the afternoon *Hauptmann* Stark took over command of the 2nd Battalion; he was formerly commander of the 6th Company."

More fresh American troops managed to penetrate the town. The battalion staff was pressurized more and more. The commander of the signals platoon, Herbert Reintal, tried to break out with his platoon. The energetic troopers, nearly all veteran paratroopers, managed to chase the Americans out of several houses. But a little while later the German paratroopers were encircled and captured. The 8th Company of *Fallschirmjäger-Regiment 9* was caught in a pincer movement. The Americans attacked from three sides.

Wartime and modern views of a house in Faymonville.

Back to Harry Pritts of the 1st Battalion of the 16th Infantry Regiment: "At 1630 hours, we went into town. Around 1700 hours the seven of us got into the second house as it was getting dark. We stayed there all night and about 0430 hours

A tank of B Company of the U.S. 738th Armored Battalion rolling forward at Faymonville. It mounts a T1E1 mine shredder. U.S. ARMY

the next morning the Germans moved out. At daybreak I went back to the field to retrieve a carton of cigarettes a buddy carried and found seventy-five to eighty men from A Company that had been killed. C Company came up to relieve us and we were sent back to regroup. The seven of us were together from then on as we fought from town to town."

By dusk the American 16th Infantry Regiment possessed half of Faymonville. Despite heavy American artillery, tank and

Two members of the U.S. 1st Infantry Division stand next to an M8 Greyhound armored car in Faymonville, 18 January 1945. U.S. ARMY

mortar fire, the German paratroopers held their positions in the southern part of Faymonville. In a further advance by the Americans in the evening, the first aid post was encircled, and the German doctor with his medics and a large number of wounded were captured. In the evening the heavily hit 2nd Battalion of *Fallschirmjäger-Regiment 9* pulled out of the village of Faymonville to the villages of Steinbach and the farm of Stefanshof located 2000 meters south of Faymonville on the road to Ondenval.

The weak forces of the 1st Battalion of *Fallschirmjäger-Regiment 9* also yielded to the ever-increasing pressure of the Americans, and by the evening had to evacuate the completely destroyed village of Thirimont. The remainder of 3rd

Company, 1st Battalion, *Fallschirmjäger-Regiment 9*, soon was encircled and captured. *Hauptmann* Schiffke, the battalion commander of the 1st Battalion of *Fallschirmjäger-Regiment 9*, was severely wounded in a leg, and in order to have a better view of the situation, had himself pulled through the terrain on a sled.

Hauptmann Heinz Fick, commander of the 2nd Company of *Fallschirmjäger-Regiment 9*, wrote in his last letter to his wife (he was killed on 20 January 1945 at the church of Amel in an American artillery barrage): "On the night of the sixteenth, after a drive of several stages that lasted several hours, I reached the billet where, on the 1st of the month I had billeted my new warrant officer. What I learned there was shocking. After the fierce attacks by the Americans, virtually nothing existed anymore of the battalion. My company—as far as it existed—was able to break out, part of it was with the neighboring 8th Regiment and the other part was with another battalion. The captain, who in my absence commanded the company, was captured, so that I have only the trains left to command; furthermore my *Bürsche* (batman) Gödke and two other fine lads reported in, and they now accompany me steadily.

"I reported to my regimental commander, *Oberst* von Hoffmann, who gave me command of the regimental reserve, a small band, which has to carry out a counterattack in case of an enemy penetration. May the All-Powerful grant me and my men success in case of an attack!

"The entire proud regiment is only a combat group now, in which majors lead 50 men, the men for days lie in the snowed woods and in holes in the earth, without being able to warm themselves, without any warm food, without relief, and yet the positions have to be held with the remainder and they will be held.

"In secret and quiet everyone thinks of fresh, strong troops. May God soon grant us a favorable change in our situation, as the troops are suffering mightily from exhaustion, yet as Prussian-raised soldiers, we are confident and hope for the best.

"At the time I am at the regimental command post and continue to learn what the situation is. There is much to say,

Additional views of the Greyhound from page 147. U.S. ARMY

but—next to me sits the *Oberst*, directly next to him is the radio, and it is a continuous coming and going, during writing I listen in on all the more-or-less loud conversations, so that it is best that I close this letter for today.

Wartime and modern views of a house in Faymonville.

U.S. ARMY/HANS WIJERS

"Regrettably the 'Santas' [idiots] of the company lying in front of me have left all my mail—which should be considerable—with the trains."

CHAPTER 17

American Attack on Steinbach and Remonval

The 18th Infantry Regiment of the 1st Infantry Division was having tough going against well-emplaced German positions in the Klingelsberg Hill to their front, but the attack pushed on. The 1st Battalion of the 18th Infantry Regiment, 1st Infantry Division, was pulled out of the attack and swung to the west to support the 23rd Infantry Regiment, of the 2nd Infantry Division.

On the left side of the American front line, the reinforced 23rd Infantry Regiment, under the command of Colonel Lovless of the 2nd Infantry Division, was in position in the Waimes area, which had been held previously by elements of the 2nd and 3rd Battalions of *Fallschirmjäger-Regiment 9*. The 23rd was to take Steinbach and Remonval. Remonval was defended by about 150 German paratroopers and Steinbach by about 100. The heights southeast of Steinbach also were held by the paratroopers. The approach routes to the villages had been mined. At the railway bridge toward Steinbach, fifty-six mines were found, to the detriment of the accompanying tanks and tank destroyers. Two tank destroyers and one tank were knocked out.

Lieutenant Covington, a platoon leader in C Company of the U.S. 741st Tank Battalion, recalls: "At about 1500 hours on 15 January, my platoon drove from the company command post in Robertville with four tanks (M4 Shermans) in the direction of Waimes. There we were to join up with the 23rd Infantry Regiment of the 2nd Infantry Division. We were to support an attack by the 1st and 2nd Battalions of the 23rd Infantry in the direction of Steinbach. Even before daylight we

This young German paratrooper seems pleased to be taken prisoner. For him the war is over. U.S. ARMY

drove our tanks into a position south of Waimes (about 900 meters) to provide direct fire on the villages of Steinbach and Removal.

"But then at about 0730 hours orders came to shift fire to a German position ('Nose') south of Steinbach. We could do this from our position, but the ground fog prevented us from seeing the results of this fire support."

Lieutenant Joseph Dew, another platoon leader in C Company of the 741st Tank Battalion, writes: "On the morning of 15 January, my platoon, consisting of four tanks, moved into the outskirts of Steinbach to clear out the Germans. We had to remove a tank destroyer from the road that had been knocked out by a mine, and moved down the road to blow up a house that was holding up the advance of the infantry. As we were moving up, one of the tanks hit a mine and was towed back to Waimes."

Lieutenant Covington continues his story: "At about 0830 hours, the 2nd Battalion of the 23rd Infantry needed two of our tanks for support of an attack on an enemy position.

Modern view of Remonval. HANS WIJERS

Together with Sergeant Fitts, I drove along to support this attack. A fortified position, consisting of two houses at a cross-roads at 'coordinate 68,' which already had twice been taken by the American 30th Infantry Division but recaptured again by the Germans, now was taken by G Company of the 23rd Infantry Regiment. About 30 Germans were captured there. Our tanks were not supposed to continue on, but an order came down from the 23rd Infantry that the attack was to be continued to the south.

"From this crossroads we turned nearly forty-five degrees to the east in the direction of Remonval. When we left 'Point 68,' we nearly drove into some minefields which had to be cleared up first. We got heavy machine gun fire on our left flank when we slowly drove towards Remonval, but due to the heavy fog we could not be sure whether it was the enemy or maybe our own troops, so that we could not open fire. At 1700 hours, the report that they had been hostile units came in, so we immediately opened fire with our tanks, and after a while the enemy machine guns were silenced in this manner.

"At about 1730 hours we drove toward Remonval-South and had direct contact with German soldiers who had taken up positions in the houses. We could see that some of these soldiers were withdrawing in a southerly direction. With our .50-caliber machine guns fixed to our tanks, we gave them a parting 'greeting.'

"About 1800 hours, two of our tanks were relieved by two tanks that had just returned from the workshops. So now we could drive back to the workshop with our two tanks. The two tanks which relieved us remained in support with the 23rd Infantry in the clearance of the village and as anti-tank support in case of enemy counterattacks."

Lieutenant Crisler, another C Company platoon leader, remembers: "On the morning of 15 January, my platoon of four tanks moved into Waimes, remaining there until the afternoon, and then we moved out to take up tank destroyer guard for the night in the vicinity of Steinbach."

Captain Young, the commander of C Company, 741st Tank Battalion, stated that during the day, the 2nd Platoon of C Company worked with G Company, 2nd Battalion, 23rd Infantry Regiment, 2nd Infantry Division, using four tanks, including the tank dozer. The dozer returned to the company area at 1200 hours on order of the commander of the 23rd Infantry Regiment, to assist the 1st Battalion of the 23rd Infantry Regiment. Sergeant Fitt's tank developed mechanical trouble soon after and was returned to the company area for repair, leaving two tanks under Lt. Covington, with G Company, 2nd Battalion, 23rd Infantry Regiment. At 1600 hours two C Company tanks relieved Lieutenant Covington and the 2nd tank, to allow them to return to Waimes to re-service. Lieutenant Dew with four tanks and Lieutenant Crisler with two tanks supported the 1st Battalion, 23rd Infantry Regiment. The tanks were returned in pairs to re-service late in the day. Three tanks were to assume antitank positions on the Faymonville–Steinbach road. The C Company tank dozer and two tank destroyers were to proceed to the town of Remonval to clear the roads. Before dawn on 16 January 1945, this dozer, supported by the tank destroyers, was to jump off and clear the road to Ondenval.

The 3rd Battalion of *Fallschirmjäger-Regiment 9* of *Hauptmann* Buchholz, could not hold up the enemy any longer and was forced to withdraw from Remonval and toward Ondenval. By 1900 hours, the Americans had taken both villages and in the process captured about 100 paratroopers. The night itself remained quiet after heavy fighting.

The next morning, 16 January 1945, the 23rd Infantry Regiment, 2nd Infantry Division, with support of tanks of the 741st Tank Battalion, tried to break through to Ondenval.

Oberschütze Rudi Frühbeisser of *Fallschirmjäger-Regiment 9* recalls: "In the afternoon of 16 January, it comes to a bitter fight with the American troops. At the crossroads of Ondenval–Eibertingen–Iveldingen (am Kreuz) and at our positions at Stephanshof we receive heavy fire out of the woods of the Rohrbusch. U.S. troops have entered the woods and try to break through our positions. Only with a counterattack we can drive the Yanks out of this wood section.

"Schwarz, who was with the 13th Company, and held their positions north of Iveldingen, is killed. The 1st Battalion has taken up new positions north of Montenau on the hillside of the valley of the Amel River.

"In the evening again, this time a bigger group, the Americans are attacking Stephanshof. Here are the positions of the 6th Company under heavy attack and they only manage with heavy losses for both side to stop the attack of the Yanks. Gegenmantel with his platoon is taken POW by the Americans.

"At the positions of the 1st Battalion, the Americans are attacking, and try to cross the Amel River. They are beaten back with losses on both sides. Losses for that day: twenty-two soldiers—three wounded, fifteen missing, three captured, one wounded (staying with the troops)."

Clement Turpin of the U.S. 23rd Infantry Regiment writes: "On 16 January 1945, our regiment was to make an attack in the Ondenval–Iveldingen Pass and secure a valley for the whole corps to pass through. On the day of the attack, they put my company in a wheat field unprotected. At daylight, the Germans saw us there and started dropping mortars. We were pinned down by artillery and a machine gun set up in a farmhouse window started mowing us down. It was bitter cold and we were laying in snow about a foot and a half deep, trying to dig holes to get into for cover. A mortar shell hit near one of our guys and he just shook the dirt off. Then a second one came in right in the same place and took his leg off. I remember his screams—we couldn't do a thing. We had a lot of other casualties. Finally, tanks with plows came in to clear the road ahead so our tanks could come in and support us.

"A medic came up there and asked the sergeant, 'Where are your casualties?' The Platoon Sergeant, my best friend, was bending on one knee to point when he was shot through the forehead and fell dead in the snow. I was the Platoon guide and next in line for the job, so I took over. When our tanks started firing, the Germans moved back. By nightfall we came to the edge of a forest and it began to snow heavily. We went up the side of a hill along the trees' edge line. We found prepared positions and one huge hole that an entire platoon could use to take cover. We occupied that position that night and we were freezing. We were trained not to make fires, not even for warmth, which would give away your position. We had no food, no extra ammunition, no radio for communication, nothing! We were on top of this hill by ourselves."

Captain Young of the 741st Tank Battalion reported that operations by C Company for the day had been as follows: Three C Company tanks (Dew's, Crisler's, and one other tank) commenced operations with the 1st Battalion of the 23rd Infantry Regiment. Lieutenant Dew's tank developed mechanical trouble in the morning and returned to the rear, leaving two tanks to work with the infantry. These two tanks were relieved at 1930 hours for re-servicing, two additional C Company tanks replacing them. All operations consisted of close support of the attacking infantry of the 1st Battalion, 23rd Infantry Regiment. The C Company tank dozer operated with the 1st Battalion, 23rd Infantry Regiment, clearing roads off

U.S. infantry moves through the
destroyed village of Steinbach. U.S. ARMY

mines all day. Lieutenant Covington, with three other C Company tanks jumped off with the 2nd Battalion of the 23rd Infantry Regiment this morning. During the course of the fighting, Lt. Covington's tank threw a track. A heavy concentration of enemy artillery prohibited dismounting to repair the vehicle track. Lieutenant Covington continued firing from his frozen position until the enemy fire lifted, then succeeded in replacing the track on the vehicle. An additional C Company tank was dispatched to Lieutenant Covington's platoon in anticipation of replacing his tank. This 5th tank remained for the day, making a total of five tanks in support of the 2nd Battalion, 23rd Infantry Regiment for the greater part of the day, at 1730 hours; Covington's platoon was relieved for re-servicing. Two C Company tanks replaced Covington's platoon, and are to remain with the 2nd Battalion, 23rd Infantry Regiment for the night. For the day's fighting there were neither casualties nor damage to vehicles.

Clement Turpin continues his story: "The next morning, 17 January 1945, we discovered that our man on outpost had been killed by a tree burst. So the Lieutenant and I went on a short reconnaissance and had gotten a few hundred feet when I saw three soldiers in white camouflage. I said, 'Lieutenant, the Germans . . .' He looked and said, 'That's F Company.' I said, 'We don't wear those black belts.' So I took aim, shot one down, and a firefight started. There were no more than thirty of us with no replacements, and we were freezing to the point where we didn't care if we lived or died.

"It was hard to see where the Germans were, so I kept yelling to the men, 'Fire low! Fire low! Fire at the base of the trees where you think they're hiding!' Then we heard this roar getting louder and louder and it was what a foot soldier fears most—a tank. As it got closer and closer, we realized that it was a Tiger tank. The tall pine trees began to bend and break under its weight and I could see its muzzle coming right at us. It looked like a monster coming through the woods, crushing the pines it its way. Then the turret turned and aimed in our direction and BOOM! It fired at us. Some of our men got up and ran. I hollered, 'Stay here and fight!' I picked up rocks and threw them at the foxholes to rally the men to fire their weapons. Our gunner had run away so one of my squad leaders and I jumped into a hole where the machine gun was. He fired away at the tank, but it did nothing. The tank kept firing and it dawned on us that we were all going to be killed if somebody didn't do something! I crawled through the woods to get our bazooka. I had been trained on the bazooka, but had never fired it with live ammunition. I looked out of the hole after he fired to see where his gun was aiming. After it fired, I got out of the hole on one knee and from behind a knocked-down limb, fired at the tank. It hit and just bounced off. I jumped back in the hole and it fired again. I got out and fired another round. I must have hit it about ten times, but I couldn't do any damage. Then out of the corner of my eye I caught movement to the side. I was on my knee ready to shoot at the tank when I whirled around with my bazooka and saw three Germans about fifty feet away. I took aim at a tree next to them and fired. The round blew the tree apart and killed them. If I had missed, they would have killed me. We were shocked when the tank backed off and retreated with its troops. When things quieted down, we got out of our holes and started counting bodies. We had lost three men, the Germans thirty-seven.

"So we stopped the tank, we stopped their attack, and we held our position. We carried our dead down to the road so their bodies would be found."

For this action, Turpin was awarded the Silver Star by Gen. Courtney Hodges. The citation reads as follows: "When an enemy tank began firing pointblank into the foxholes, Sergeant Turpin secured a rocket launcher and while subject to intense small arms fire, crawled through the dense woods to within fifty yards of his target, firing his weapon until the tank was forced to withdraw. This action allowed the men to concentrate their fire upon the enemy infantry to their front. Then, Sergeant Turpin, at a range of twenty yards, killed three enemy infantrymen with the rocket launcher. This bold initiative and gallant action were an important factor in repelling the enemy drive."

Captain Young, commander of C Company of the 741st Tank Battalion, reported that operations by C Company for the day had been as follows: Two C Company tanks had remained with 1st Battalion, 23rd Infantry Regiment during the night (plans for four tanks to remain with 1st Battalion had been modified). Young further stated that at 1100 hours, Lieutenant Crisler, with two tanks reported to 1st Battalion, making a total of four now operating with that battalion. Lieutenant Covington, with four tanks, had reported at 0630 hours to 2nd Battalion, 23rd Infantry Regiment. The C Company tank dozer returned to the company command post the night of 16 January, after having been used for clearing roads in the forward area. The dozer remains on alert.

Young reported that Covington was operating with four tanks with the 2nd Battalion and that Crisler was operating with four tanks with the 3rd Battalion. These units jumped off at 1500 hours moving south of Ondenval to secure the roads. At 1550 hours, instructions were received by Captain Young from the commander of the 23rd Infantry Regiment to notify Covington's tanks to cease fire and move to the vicinity of Ondenval and await a call there from either the 3rd or 1st Battalion, 23rd Infantry Regiment. C Company, 741st Tank Battalion, had three tanks and the tank dozer available for use at the C Company tank park.

CHAPTER 18

Heavy Fighting for Schoppen

Under the command of *Oberstleutnant* Schenk, *Kampfgruppe Schenk* was formed from a platoon of the engineer company of *Regiment 8* and other elements, such as five assault tanks of *Sturmpanzer-Battalion 217* (*Sturmpanzer IV Brummbär's*) and three assault guns. This battle group was to prove a valuable support for *Fallschirmjäger-Regiment 9*. The combat group remained under the command of the regimental commander, *Oberst i.G.* Helmut von Hoffmann.

Lance Corporal "Smiling Al" Alvarez of C Company of the American 16th Infantry Regiment, writes: "The morning of 15 January dawned crisp and sunny, and Lieutenant Cangelosi returned from battalion briefing: 'We are going to take Schoppen, the next town to the southeast. Let's move it.' Trudging again through the snow, we encountered some woods where heavy machine-gun fire erupted. Lieutenant Cangelosi quieted it with a high-explosive concentration. We held up in these woods with no fires, no hot chow, and tried stomping our feet to stay warm all night. It seemed that we were now in reserve, since the 2nd Battalion was in the lead."

On the morning of 16 January, at about 0915 hours, when the American soldiers of the 16th Infantry Regiment of the 1st Infantry Division entered Faymonville to advance in the direction of Schoppen, it became clear that the paratroopers had withdrawn from the town and taken up positions farther to south. When F Company of the 16th Infantry advanced down the road toward Schoppen, they were fired on by light infantry weapons, assault guns and assault tanks of *Kampfgruppe Schenk*.

In the Rohr woods, below Hill 533, a heavy battle took place.

Karl Egon Liebach, who commanded
Fallschirmjäger-Regiment 8 after 11 January.

The after-action report of F Company, 16th Infantry Regiment, gives the following information on a battle that claimed many casualties on both sides: "16 January 1945. Company arose at 0300 hours, had breakfast and moved out at 0500 hours. Went into the attack with no trouble. Germans brought up tanks which fired upon the men. Friendly artillery fire also caused some casualties. Woods very thick and dark. Snow suits made Germans and Americans unrecognizable to each other, until only a few feet apart. About 1900 hours, moved back nearer town. 8 EM LWA; 2 EM, SWA."

Rainer Bender of *Kampfgruppe Schenk* writes: "At first we fought in the so-called 'Rohr-wood' at the slope of the hill and inflicted large losses on the Yanks. In the night one of our officers disappeared, I think he was *Oberleutnant* Wedding. At dawn we saw him again, mostly with American food, and once with two 'walkie-talkie's' (radios) which he had taken off the Yanks."

North of Iveldingen, in the area held by the 13th Company of *Fallschirmjäger-Regiment 9*, a heavy withdrawal battle took place. The company commander, *Oberleutnant* Dr. Helmuth Weihe, was unable to hold up the continually assaulting Americans for very long. Seventeen men were missing. The withdrawal clearly showed that the Americans were determined to get into Schoppen. 800 meters to the west of Schoppen on the road to Faymonville, exactly opposite Hill 548 on the left there was a small wood.

There, however, the Americans were beaten back by *Kampfgruppe Schenk*. The assault tanks and assault guns were firing at will in the woods. The reinforced American 23rd Infantry Regiment of the 2nd Infantry Division (with the attached 18th Infantry Regiment of the 1st Infantry Division in support) prepared an assault on Schoppen. When at 0730 hours the American soldiers were preparing for their own assault in a wood west of Schoppen, *Kampfgruppe Schenk* attacked the completely surprised Americans.

With about 200 paratroopers of *Fallschirmjäger-Regiment 8* (160 men just had arrived as reinforcements from Holland) and 60 paratroopers of the 13th Company of *Fallschirmjäger-Regiment 6*, as well as 30 men of the reconnaissance unit of the *3rd Fallschirmjäger Division*, supported by the eight (the American war diary mentions seven) assault tanks and assault guns, the Americans, after bitter fighting that lasted until the afternoon, were thrown out of the woods by *Kampfgruppe Schenk*. When the paratroopers went into the woods after the battle, they found 150 dead Americans. From this day on, the paratroopers called these woods the "Wood of the Dead."

On 19 January 1945, the regimental command post once again was located in the Möderscheider Mill in the valley. At dawn, a fight with stragglers took place at the Vieux Mühle at the river Amel. Platoon commander Rudolf Banersoi was wounded there. *Oberleutnant* Michel, commander of the 15th

Pioneer Company, Banersoi, and two troopers were missing since the fight began. The regimental front ran from south of Schoppen over Hill 534 to Hill 533 (the so-called Eibertinger heights) to the Bambusch Wood to Mirfeld and Amel.

On 20 January 1945 at 0730 hours, the Americans attacked without any artillery preparation. There was such a strong snowdrift that one could not see 100 meters, which kept the German assault guns and assault tanks from being effective; they would have had to shoot "blind." The American attack took place with tank support from the north, west, and east. The part of *Kampfgruppe Schenk* north of Schoppen was ordered to withdraw to the southern part of the town. Telephone and radio connections to the regiments were broken off. *Kampfgruppe Schenk* planned to wage a withdrawal battle to the Möderscheider Mill. The command post of *Kampfgruppe Schenck* was withdrawn from Schoppen when the Americans were only 100 meters distant. The withdrawal took place in an orderly fashion, and by 1000 hours, *Kampfgruppe Schenk* was located at Hill 534 at the crossroads underneath the Eibertinger Heights.

Orders then came down from the *3rd Fallschirmjäger-Division* that Schoppen was to be retaken immediately. *Kampfgruppe Schenk* was assured reinforcements of extra troops and artillery support. After a short briefing the paratroopers prepared themselves. Under command of the energetic company commander, *Oberleutnant* Wedding, they managed to penetrate Schoppen again. There were seven assault guns and assault tanks with the paratroopers. During the fighting, characterized by indescribable harshness, the paratroopers managed to capture forty Americans, which were immediately brought back to the starting point, and several American tanks were destroyed. But pressure from the Americans increased so that Kampfgruppe Schenk, which had managed to break in, once more had to withdraw to the southern edge of Schoppen. In the battle, Wedding was killed.

Parts of *Fallschirmjäger-Regiment 5* were involved in the battle, as recounted by Rolf Odendahl: "Around the second half of January 1945, we received orders to change again our

Rainer Bender.

positions, and we took up our new positions along the forest ridge near Schoppen. Our old positions close to the firebreak in Bütgenbacher Heck are still to be seen today."

"Around the nineteenth of January—I can't remember the exact day—our unit was involved in an attack on the American positions close to Schoppen. The attack was a disaster and I lost a lot of good men. The next day Schoppen was taken by the American troops.

"A few days later the Americans captured at bright daylight two of my men from an machine gun position, who were located in a forward area of the forest. They had their machineguns aimed in the direction of Schoppen. I was going to have a look at the situation with them, all I found was an abandoned machine gun. These men were all of a sudden bypassed by an American patrol and captured. At that time their disappearance was a mystery.

"Months later, when we were already in captivity in the USA, one of the gunners spoke to me during the moment we received our daily food and explained to me how it had come to the surprising capture. Feint attacks were run and suddenly from the front were the two that had turned their attention forward, threatened from the back with rifles and prompted to surrender. We had noticed nothing of everything because of the dense forest."

At 1200 hours, a new order came down from the *3rd Fallschirmjäger-Division*: "Schoppen is to be evacuated again!"

Rainer Bender of *Kampfgruppe Schenk* writes: "Via radio orders now came in that we were to withdraw on Schoppen and to defend this place till dusk. When Schoppen was finally captured by the Americans on 21 January 1945, we withdrew to Möderscheid. But before we withdrew from Schoppen, we first in secure cover sang the song: 'Jenseits des Tales' ['On the Other Side of the Valley']. The Americans took revenge with powerful mortar salvoes. During our retreat there was a lot of snow."

When the paratroopers again reached the starting point of their attack, the *Kampfgruppe*, not counting the assault guns and the assault tanks, consisted of only twelve troopers.

The Americans launched four large-scale attacks on Hill 534 which were repulsed in a bloody manner each time. Man-to-man fighting for the slope continued until the evening. For a long time, one could hear the wounded Americans cry in front of the positions.

Rainer Bender continues: "On arrival in Möderscheid, we immediately had to dig in at the northwestern edge of the village. That was an exertion to the utmost in the snowstorm. During the next days we held our positions on the route of attack toward Schoppen with machine guns and bazookas."

On 19 January 1945, four more German-held towns were taken in the worst weather of this campaign. Eibertingen, the first town, was defended by a force of about 130 replacements and stragglers from the Rohrbusch. Entrance to the town was blocked by a large number of wooden box-mines. Assault guns

Isaac Wilmer Jumper, one of the men of
the 16th Infantry Division killed in the
attack. CAROL JUMPER MERCER

and one *Sturmpanzer* (15cm) were in town which faced the
23rd Infantry Regiment. It was only after heavy artillery concentrations forced the Germans to fall back into the town that
the infantry was able to move forward and seize several houses
on the northern edge of town.

The Germans counterattacked immediately and bitter
hand-to-hand fighting resulted. By 1400 hours, the Germans
began to pull out of Deidenberg. Many prisoners were taken
and many dead Germans were counted in the streets of Deidenberg.

The towns of Montenau and Iveldingen, also taken by the
23rd Infantry Regiment put up less resistance and only twenty-
two prisoners were taken from these two towns. During this
battle for Iveldingen, Capt. Charles B. MacDonald, commander of I Company of the 3rd Battalion of the U.S. 23rd
Infantry Regiment of the 2nd Infantry Division was wounded.

A B-26 Marauder crew of the U.S. Ninth Air Force visits the Schoppen area. Here they examine an M10 tank destroyer.

The B-26 crew leaves the area in a Weasel.

Members of I Company of the 16th Infantry Regiment ride a tank into Schoppen. U.S. ARMY

One of the knocked-out *Brummbär* of *Kampfgruppe Schenk*, near Möderscheid. U.S. ARMY

More withdrawals of the 13th Company, *Fallschirmjäger-Regiment 9* followed. All along the front, paratroopers of the *3rd Fallschirmjäger-Division* were embroiled in bitter defensive battles with American units. Now the paratroopers of the 13th Company, who were still at the defense line Halbacher–Mühle

Two views of Deidenberg, taken by the U.S. 23rd Infantry Regiment after heavy fighting.

southwest from Iveldingen are trying to get back the *Fallschirmjäger-Regiment 9*. The succeed to get back to the new frontline positions near Mirfeld at the Möderscheider Bach, where they are getting back to the *Fallschirmjäger-Regiment 9.*

CHAPTER 19

The Attack on the Morsheck Crossroads on 24 January 1945

On 22 January 1945, where the front line essentially ran from Deidenberg through Eibertingen to Schoppen, the attack of the determined 1st Infantry Division was made primarily by rearranging its forces and eliminating particularly stubbornly defended sections in the front.

The *3rd Fallschirmjäger-Division*, along with the 89th Infantry Division, was involved in heavy fighting with much better equipped American troops along their entire front. One of these particularly fiercely defended sections was the woodland Bütgenbacher Heck, where parts of the 89th Infantry Division of Maj. Gen. Walter Bruns were well prepared for the enemy in defense since the end of December 1944. The 1st Infantry Division succeeded despite intense fire from small arms and artillery fire to clean out about 800 yards from the northern edge of the forest in worst weather and terrain conditions of the enemy.

In the other sections of the front German troops took a small breather further and strengthening existing defensive positions on 24 January to the reorganizing of their units and the hasty construction.

The crossroads of Morsheck was of great importance for the U.S. troops. Here was one of the few usable roads from the north between Büllingen and St. Vith, and at the same time, it was one of the few still usable supply lines for the German troops to its front in this section. From the German side, the road was covered by artillery, by mortar, and also by an infantry company, which had to keep this important point, whatever the costs.

The 1st Battalion of the 26th Infantry Regiment of the 1st Infantry Division received the order to capture the crossroads at Morsheck.

Private First Class Rocco J. Moretto of C Company, 26th Infantry Regiment, 1st Infantry Division, recalls: "Finally, on 22 January 1945, after being in position for thirty-six days, the 1st Battalion, 26th Infantry Regiment, was assigned the mission to capture and hold the Morsheck crossroads. The crossroads was a vital piece of real estate as it was being used as a supply route and for the movement of troops and equipment into the Ardennes salient and the Siegfried Line.

"The area was heavily defended by self propelled guns, tanks, artillery and mortars and an oversized company of German Infantry. The attack was to take place on 24 January and C Company was relieved and taken out of the defensive line at Dom Bütgenbach on 22 January and moved back to Bütgenbach where we would get a good night's rest, receive equipment such as shoe packs, camouflage snow suits and a half-pound of dynamite for each man to be used for breaking up the frozen ground so that the men could more easily dig their foxholes in the shortest possible time after securing their objective.

"C Company's assignment was to take the crossroads. Captain Donald Lister, commander of C Company immediately organized a patrol for the night of 22 January which consisted of sixteen men and one officer. A radio operator carrying an SCR-300 set was also included and he would stay in touch with the main body and transmit all pertinent information as it was gathered.

"The patrol was instructed to scout the area and C Company was assigned to attack on 24 January. They would carry mostly automatic weapons and two hand grenades each.

"The patrol went out at 2200 hours and after several hours returned with the following information: The snow in some places was four feet deep. The enemy had a series of dugouts which were probably used as strong points approximately 100 yards north of the north-south road. It was believed that these positions were occupied because there were footpaths in the snow leading to the dugouts. Antitank mines were observed approximately 350 yards north of the crossroads on the north south road. This road would not be passable for vehicles until it was cleared of the mines.

"Armed with the above information, Captain Lister laid out his plan of attack and at 1800 hours on 23 January assembled his platoon leaders and key personnel to give them their respective assignments and last minute instructions."

"The time of attack was set for 0300 hours on 24 January 1945. The company was to be awakened at 0100, would receive a hot meal and last minute instructions. The 1st Platoon was assigned the point and were to attack straight down the north south road moving as quickly as the situation would permit making as little noise as possible. It was very likely the enemy would fire all their prearranged fire missions immediately as soon as we were observed.

"Upon reaching the crossroads the 1st Platoon was then to swing to the east, clear out a patch of woods and take positions on the other side of the wooded area. There they would eventually tie in with the 2nd and 3rd Platoons. The 2nd Platoon, led by Lt. Leon P. Kowalski, was instructed to follow the 1st platoon and continue down the road after the 1st had swung to the east and clean out a house just east of the crossroads. At that location they were to tie in with the 1st platoon on the east and B Company on the west.

"The 3rd Platoon would be held in reserve and would not be committed until the situation required it. If all went according to plan they would tie in with the 1st on the east and bend around to the north thereby protecting C Company's flank and rear. The weapons platoon led by Lt. Marlin Brockette were to quickly set up their mortars in battery 300 yards northeast of the crossroads and be available to fire missions in support of the rifle platoons.

"Captain Lister also attached one section of heavy machine guns to the 1st Platoon and one section of light machine guns to the 2nd Platoon. Four tanks were assigned to the company and would be available to give support after the objective was secured and the mines were cleared.

"In addition, one antitank gun would be available and could be called on to assist. Additionally, our 33rd Field Artillery had a liaison officer at 1st Battalion headquarters so we could fire missions through him.

"At 0200 hours, after breakfast and last-minute orders, the men of C Company started out from Bütgenbach and marched the approximate three miles to the line of departure at Dom Bütgenbach and prior to our arrival at Dom Bütgenbach the Company took a ten-minute break.

"At 0300, we started out in what was the coldest weather that I'd ever experienced in my whole lifetime. It was so cold the snowsuits were frozen stiff and crackled as you moved. The 1st Platoon led by Lieutenant Brooks sent out the point consisting of one squad and a second squad out as flank protection. The snowsuits blended in perfectly with the snow as they moved down the road and no opposition was met until the 1st Platoon swung to the east.

"At that point, they were met with fire from two machine guns and about a squad of riflemen. We very quickly gained fire superiority killing four of the enemy and six were taken prisoner. They were quickly disarmed and passed back to the rear.

"The 2nd Platoon in the meantime ran into enemy around the house and after a brief firefight two were killed and five more were captured. Additional Germans were caught in their dugouts and surrendered without firing a shot. As a matter of fact, they were in dugouts they had heated with cans of sterno and even had taken their boots off for more comfort. They probably never expected an attack under such horribly cold conditions.

"It was a textbook attack. Everything broke right and just as dawn was beginning to break C Company was sitting right on its objective. The men quickly started to dig in using the TNT to help break up the frozen ground. Everything was going beautifully but the TNT threw up heavy black smoke in the explosion areas. The enemy observing this quickly began to rake our positions with heavy concentrations of fire and we began to sustain heavy casualties.

"Lieutenant Kowalski, leader of the 2nd Platoon, was painfully injured from the dynamite blast and limped his way back to the Medics. He was patched up and later returned to the battle. At 1600 hours, the Germans launched a counter attack in Battalion force after a twenty-minute barrage of artillery fire. The 2nd Platoon was taking the brunt of the counter attack. When Lieutenant Kowalski returned from the medics he discovered that most of the platoon was gone. Platoon Sgt. Bob Wright had been killed. Clayton Goode, the platoon guide, had taken over, and he and Lieutenant Kowalski began directing artillery fire. One of the two machine guns was still operable but the ammunition boxes had taken a hit by artillery. Only the gunner from the original two machine guns and their crews remained and he was hand feeding the ammo from a broken machine gun belt and he almost singly handedly held off the Germans. Our artillery and mortars took care of the rest catching the Germans out in the open.

"In the meantime reinforcements were being sent to the 2nd Platoon and they were able to plug the gap and the day was saved. A second counter attack was expected but fortunately it never came. The Germans were also sustaining heavy casualties. The rest of the 1st Battalion had also taken their objectives and after a few days we were able to attack our way out of the salient and were on our way to reducing the so called Bulge. After a few weeks of almost daily attacks our lines were restored to what they were originally. While things got a little easier, we still had that horrible weather to contend with."

CHAPTER 20

Retreat of the *3rd Fallschirmjäger-Division* to a New Defense Line

*O*berschütze Rudi Frühbeisser of *Fallschirmjäger-Regiment 9* recalls: "On the morning of 24 January 1945, it comes to a long and heavy fight with American troops at Hill 523. At the same time the Americans attack the town of Möderscheid. The town is still defended by elements of *Fallschirmjäger-Regiment 5*. After a heavy fight, the brave paratroopers have to give up Möderscheid."

During the night, elements of *Fallschirmjäger-Regiment 5* tried to break out in the direction of the twin villages of Heppenbach–Halenfeld. Now the new line of defense was located 300 meters west of the little town of Heppenbach.

The twenty-fifth and twenty-sixth of January remained relatively "quiet." Only occasionally was there enemy artillery fire. Also during these two days, *Fallschirmjäger-Regiment 9* suffered casualties. During an artillery barrage on the paratroopers, Buck of the 5th Company was killed. In the 7th Company, located near Mirfeld, Poppre died from injuries suffered during an attack.

Platoon commander Rolf Odendahl of the 1st Company, *Fallschirmjäger-Regiment 5*, remembers: "On 25 or 26 January— I'm not sure now which day it was—we were released and received orders to move to Heppenbach were we would have a small break from the fighting's. I had the orders to wait for the new unit to arrive, and then go myself to Heppenbach.

"After briefing the new unit, I made myself on my way to Heppenbach. I still remember that I was very tired because of the fighting's of the last weeks and hardly getting any sleep. I was very happy that I arrived at the new location, a little pension in Heppenbach. But unfortunately having a 'break' here from the battle, which was impossible. After we had moved out from our previous positions, the Americans already had broken through and captured the forest part. We received new orders to go to a prepared line of defense in the field in front of Heppenbach.

"The position consisted of one large earth bunker, with room for two platoons and their commanders, a total of fifteen men including the two platoon leaders. In a smaller earth bunker next to it was our company commander, a *Leutnant.*

"A few days ago, we had received a few replacements. Very young soldiers and old men from the air force. They had hardly any battle experience, not even had a 'training' how to use a gun! Most of them only were interested to survive the war. We, the platoon commanders, had difficulty refraining from showing them that the battle—yes, even the war—was lost.

"The terrain consisted of rectangular meadows which were limited on all sides by hedges, thus creating a kind of ravines in between. Our earth bunker was buried at a crossroads of this sunken roads. A further junction, which was secured through mines was about thirty meters before the crossing. The pioneers had there a shield with the inscription: 'Warning! Mines!' attached. I pointed out to the company commander that the American term for mines was also 'Mines,' and when I later passed the sign as a prisoner, Americans were digging up the mines, pointing and smiling at the sign.

"In addition to our two bunkers, we had raised one machine-gun position for assurance and as a kind of extra cover behind one of the hedges. Because our company commander had found one of the men asleep during a check, we had to check the post every hour. On the day before, we had received orders to change positions and both platoon commanders received a sketch with the new positions and the roads leading to it. But the order to move out was held for another twenty-four hours. For our convenience we had packed the heavy equipment because of the high snow on a sled, including bazookas and ammunition boxes. Unfortunately we forgot to unpack it again."

"Early in the morning, still in the dark, I had finished just my post control and went back into the bunker to warm up, when one of the posts in the bunker came and reported that he had observed many Americans in the area. I went without my weapon immediately outside and alerted the company commander. He immediately recognized the hopelessness of our location and disappeared around the corner of hedges. I recognized thirty yards in front of us an enemy half-track with infantry. Until then, still no one had fired a shot.

"I grabbed the *Panzerfaust* to knock out the enemy half-track. Since many accidents happened with the *Panzerfausts*, the shooters had to keep the ignition cartridge separate from it. I checked and saw that the cartridge was missing. Quickly, I went down in the bunker where the rest of my team was and asked the shooter the cartridge. It was however a big mess in the bunker, since all their weapons and equipment were thrown together. In the meantime, we heard the first Americans shouting outside the bunker: 'Come out!' The officer glanced outside and said: 'We are surrounded, it's hopeless!' One climbed out after the other down the stairs with raised hands outside, where the Americans were around the bunker. Because I went without coat and gun into the bunker, I was looking to get my stuff together.

"To my surprise the Americans were no longer concerned with the bunker in the believe all came out. I was now alone and was wondering whether I should stay to sneak at night to my own positions. While I stood at the top of the stairs and saw outside the bunker an American with his back to me. When I stepped up a level of the stairs to go higher it must have made a noise and this noise must have made the post turned around. He aimed his gun at me and shouted: 'Come out!' Carefully, I handed out my pistol and raised my hands."

Oberschütze Rudi Frühbeisser of *Fallschirmjäger-Regiment 9* remembers: "On 28 January 1945, orders from *Fallschirmjäger-Regiment 5* came to move to a new line of defense. New line of defense: the high grounds at the road Heppenbach–Honsfeld!

"In the early morning, the Americans with strong units attacked Hepscheid. Strong enemy forces were attacking our neighbor, the 3rd Battalion of *Fallschirmjäger-Regiment 5*. For the moment, there is a big gap in our front line.

"We were supposed to move out before darkness set in and we can cross the high ground east of Halenfeld. But the order to move out came too late. At around 2000 hours, the order finally came. In darkness *Fallschirmjäger-Regiment 9* and the battle group tried to get out. All contacts with other units were lost because the Americans were already on the road to Honsfeld. They already moved in between the battle group and our headquarters.

"Only at night was it possible to establish contact with other units. We now built a new defense line. It went from Rodenberg and Hill 623 to south of Honsfeld. The strength of the battle group was between sixty and seventy men. The night stays quite."

Oberschütze Dieter Kutschera of the 8th Company of the 2nd Battalion of *Fallschirmjäger-Regiment 8* recollects: "We were released and moved to Heppenbach. On 28 January, the Americans attacked Morsheck. When we attacked near to Heppenbach, a friend, Platoon Commander Schneiders, a few other paratroopers, and I were wounded. The wounded ones who were still able to walk, myself included, had to walk back to Losheimergraben."

On 29 January 1945, before midday, the paratroopers tried to move back again. A new line of defense was built near the street from Holzheim–Honsfeld. It ran through a forest called Schur–Busch. The American units who were pushing the Germans back more and more finally got to Hill 623. In the afternoon, the Americans renewed their heavy attack on Holzheim. This time the paratroopers of *Fallschirmjäger-Regiment 5* had to give up Holzheim.

The retreat out of Holzheim by the Germans was chaos. All connections were lost. During the fighting that followed in the forest, one paratrooper was wounded, twenty-two went missing, and sixteen were captured by the Americans. There was no contact to any of the other units in the area. In darkness the remaining paratroopers moved back across the Frankenbach creek to Lanzerath.

From 30 January, the remaining German paratroopers tried to break out and reach a new line of defense behind Losheimergraben near the German border. Since the early morning, a heavy attack took place along the whole German defense line. *Fallschirmjäger-Regiment 9* (about 450 men) and *Kampfgruppe Schenk* (about 40 men) were able to hold the lines at first. Close to the German defense line were three Sherman tanks that were knocked out and fifty to sixty American soldiers who were killed during the heavy fighting.

Frühbeisser continues: "We received message from our headquarters: enemy in strength of two or three companies are going through the forest directly to our headquarters! Just about 150 meters away!! We don't have any radio contact anymore, so orders are given to breakout!"

For *Kampfgruppe Schenck*, which was surrounded by the Americans, a very adventurous operation started. The battle group was trying to break out under the cover of the Büllinger forest with its remaining twenty-five men. They are taking the wounded soldiers with them. *Fallschirmjäger-Regiment 9* retreated to Lanzerath. They arrived there in the evening, totally beaten.

The road to Lanzerath and the German border was already closed of to *Kampfgruppe Schenk* by American troops. After a difficult march through knee-deep snow, the *Kampfgruppe* reaches a point 500 meters south of the station of Losheimergraben.

Nobody of the *Kampfgruppe* thought that it would be the end, that they had no way out. The remaining men—now sixteen in all—were depending on the knowledge of the veteran leaders in the group. *Hauptmann* Stark assured the youngsters that they will find a way out. In a little ditch near the railroad, Stark gave his men a little break. Then forward again. He moved his men underneath a railroad bridge in the direction of Losheimergraben. Not long after they left their position, enemy artillery fire fell down on it.

The *Kampfgruppe* took up positions northwest of Losheimergraben near the road to Hünningen. Next to them was *Infanterie-Regiment 1055* of the *89th Infanterie-Division*. They had already met this regiment during the fighting for Düren. Ten more men of the 13th Company, under the command of *Oberleutantn* Weihe, found their way out.

Rainer Bender remembers: "A breakthrough to the *3rd Fallschirmjäger-Division* was impossible. After a while some stragglers of the 13th Company found their way to us and together we sneaked away through Udenbreth in the direction of our pillbox defense line in the forest of Udenbreth. I was covering our retreat with my MG 42 and when we came to cross a fire break, we received heavy fire from Americans who tried to block our way out."

On 31 January, parts of *Fallschirmjäger-Regiment 9* were still fighting in Lanzerath. There the Americans nearly captured the regimental commander, *Oberst i.G.* von Hoffmann. With only about 450 soldiers, the regiment retreated back into the forest close to Frauenkron behind the *Westwall*.

After that, *Kampfgruppe Schenk* fought its way through with its last twelve paratroopers in the direction of Udenbreth. On 31 January, totally exhausted and starving, they finally reached the little town of Schorrenberg, which had been completely leveled. There they received for the first time in many days a warm meal and were able to find a warm spot in the basement of some of the damaged houses and finally get some sleep.

Sturmpanzer-Abteilung 217, in support of *Kampfgruppe Schenk* with several *Sturmpanzer* and assault guns, retreated through Lanzerath at the end of January.

The headquarters of the *3rd Fallschirmjäger-Division* was already in Jünkerath (Germany) on 31 January. Elements of *Fallschirmjäger-Regiment 5* could hold Losheimergraben for several days and even Losheim until 5 February 1945. But here came an end to the Battle of the Bulge for the *3rd Fallschirmjäger-Division*. It had been a tough battle and the *3rd Fallschirmjäger-Division* had lost many men during the battle.

CHAPTER 21

Captured!

Many of the paratroopers of the *3rd Fallschirmjäger-Division* were captured during the operations of the American forces in 1945.

Platoon commander Rolf Odendahl of the 1st Company, *Fallschirmjäger-Regiment 5*, describes his experience: "When I was taken prisoner in Heppenbach, I was transported to Möderscheid for interrogation. It went like this: An American soldier appeared and said that he was an German communist and was immigrated to the USA. He was now ready to interrogate us. Those who wouldn't talk would be shot!

"We, the two platoon commanders, still had the drawings with us from our new positions. We quickly agreed on a moment to turn around and pee against the wall, drop the little papers, and quickly put snow over it with our feet.

"Then he took one of the younger soldiers out of my unit. He walked along the other platoon commander, who was upset about the way this American soldier treated us. '*Du Schwein.*' Then the American soldier shouted at me, 'Shut up you!' I said, 'I didn't say a word,' and the other platoon commander said, 'I was the one who said it.' Then the American soldier replied again, 'You also should shut up!'

"He took the young soldier behind the house. After a few moments, we heard several shots being fired. Then the American soldier came back alone. He said, 'He didn't wanted to talk, so I shot him. The next one who won't say anything will go the same way.' And then he took another soldier behind the house. After a while the American soldier returned again with the young paratrooper and gave us some freedom to stand in a barn. He was giving us some cigarettes, and suddenly the one supposedly killed was back also! He told us that the American solder had fired in the air and kept him under guard when the American walked back to us.

"I can say that we were treated very fair by the American front troops who captured us. But when we were interrogated in a later phase by troops behind the front, we were constantly threatened. The way they treated us than was not very 'friendly.' On the way by train from Attichy / Frankreich to St. Mere Eglise, we got beaten up badly by an American MP. We had twelve men that were wounded badly. But after that we were treated fair, and I must say when we were send to the USA, the civilians were very friendly to us. Nothing happened anymore."

Leonhardt Maniura of the 15th Pioneer Company of *Fallschirmjäger-Regiment 9* remembers: "When I came on 14 January in U.S. captivity, I did hide my gun with the idea to be able to get it back soon. We took off our belt and stuff and went out on demand of the Americans. I had to go out as the first soldier. Americans were already at the door, we had not believed that they were so skin close to us. They tore me the steel helmet from the head. The other soldiers immediately took their helmets off. It was weird to see that most Americans had their guns mounted with rifle grenades. I could not remember that we had been fired on with such grenades in the farmyard. Maybe this was lost in the sound of the battle.

"We took our wounded with us on wooden doors out of the damaged houses. As we marched on, we observed a V1 on the opposite slope of the mountain 'Haute Sarts' going down. If we all quickly went to cover, I can't tell, anyway, it was only about 200 meters to the point of impact. We were very lucky, because the V1 did not explode! We—and also the American soldiers—were all paralyzed of the shock.

"Then we walked along on the right side of the impact area in the direction of Sedan, and we came on a nice long alley that was leading us in a northly direction, in the direction of Baugnez. On this road—we prisoners of war with our hands up—our own troops were still firing with artillery and mortars (we left the wounded on our way at an American aid station) and they exploded sometime not really that far from us, like if they wanted to say 'good-bye'! We were really mad on our own soldiers! They could see us with hands in the air, and know that we were 'friendly' troops? When we marched on, we came to a crossroad, were we saw dead, partly covered with snow laying alongside the road. Now we were ordered to walk back and for along the dead American soldier, still with our arms in the air. A one star American General came up to us and screamed. Is this justice? Is this justice what your friends of the SS did?? And all the time we were filmed and pictures were taken from us.

"I thought, well this is your last moment, this is it, I had my mind completely empty and could only think that they were going to shoot us. Also because when I looked again to the star on the American general's helmet, I thought it is a Russian commissar, because that star looked about the same. But nothing happened to us.

"We were surprised that just directly behind the front line so many press people were around, along with high-ranking U.S. officers. I never had seen that at our own side. So now I am a prisoner of war, and not going for a short 'holiday' back home as promised. But that wouldn't have been a nice 'holiday' anyway, as the Russians now occupied Beuthen in Oberschlesien. I was not listed as missing, but, as I heard after the war from the WAST in Berlin, as having transferred to the *5th Fallschirmjäger-Division*!"

Sources

After-Action Reports, 18th Infantry Regt. (1st Inf. Div.), December 1944.

After-Action Reports, 16th Infantry Regt. (1st Inf. Div.), December 1944.

After-Action Report, 120th Infantry Regiment (30th Inf. Div.).

After-Action Report, 119th Infantry Regiment (30th Inf. Div.).

After-Action Report, 741st Tank Battalion.

The Bridgehead Sentinel (newspaper of the 1st Infantry Division Association).

Combat Interviews of the 1st Infantry Division.

18th Regiment History, December 1944.

1st Division G-1 Report, December 1944.

1st Division G-2 Report, December 1944.

1st Inf Division Artillery Report, December 1944.

First United States Army Report of Operations (20 October 1943–1 August 1944).

First United States Army Report of Operations (1 August 1944–22 February 1945).

Gara, William B., and Charles C. Diggs. "Mine Laying Operations in the Ardennes. *Military Review* 25 (February 1946): 63–67.

Knickerbocker, H. R. *Danger Forward: The Story of the First Division in WWII.* Washington, DC: Zenger, 1979.

Kriegsschicksale 1944–1945.

Pulver, Murray S. *The Longest Year.* Sioux Falls, SD: Pine Hill Press, 1986.

Reports, 5th, 7th, 32d, 33d and 955th FA Bns, December 1944.

Roppelt, Fritz. *Der Vergangenheit auf der Spur: 3. Fallsch.Jg.Division.* Self-published, 1993.

16th Regiment History, December 1944.

The 30th Infantry Division Association (Frank Towers).

Wijers, Hans. *Ziel die Maas.*

WEBSITES

www.30thinfantry.org

www.oldhickory30th.com

Acknowledgments

It is nearly impossible to list all the people who helped with the book, though forgetting only one is unforgivable. To all the veterans, relatives, co-historians, and others who have contributed, I give thanks with all of my heart. I especially want to thank a few very special friends, without whose help I would never have been able to write the book: Karl-Heinz Heck, my guide in Belgium, who took me to places hardly anyone else could have found and provided me with seldom-seen photos from his collection; B. O. Wilkins (K Company, 393rd Infantry Regiment, 99th Infantry Division); Frank van de Bergh, my Dutch colleague and friend (who sadly died way to early), who did many of the German-to-English translations; Frank Rieser, who made some wonderful drawings; and Warren Watson, who permitted me the use of his site, which is dedicated to his father and his fellow brave comrades. Thanks also to Heinrich Gideons, who sent me all the letters of his father, *Hauptmann* Heinrich Fick, and to Carol Jumper for the photo of her father and for all her efforts to help me find more from her father's outfit.

Stackpole Military History Series

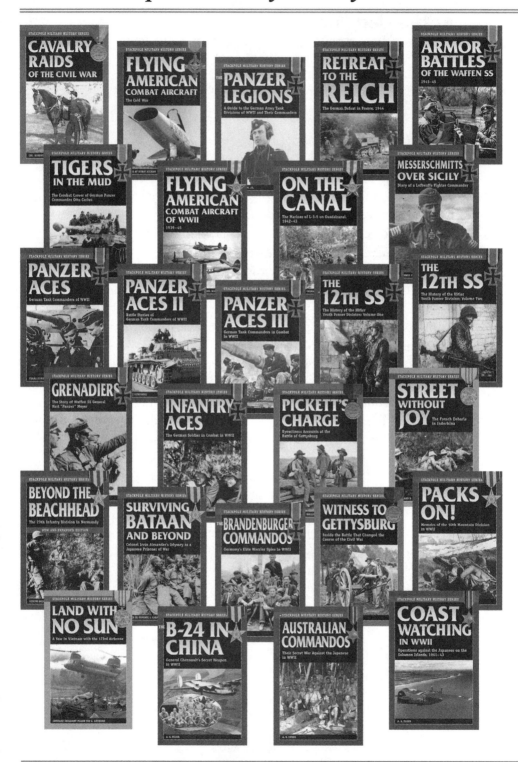

Real battles. Real soldiers. Real stories.

Stackpole Military History Series

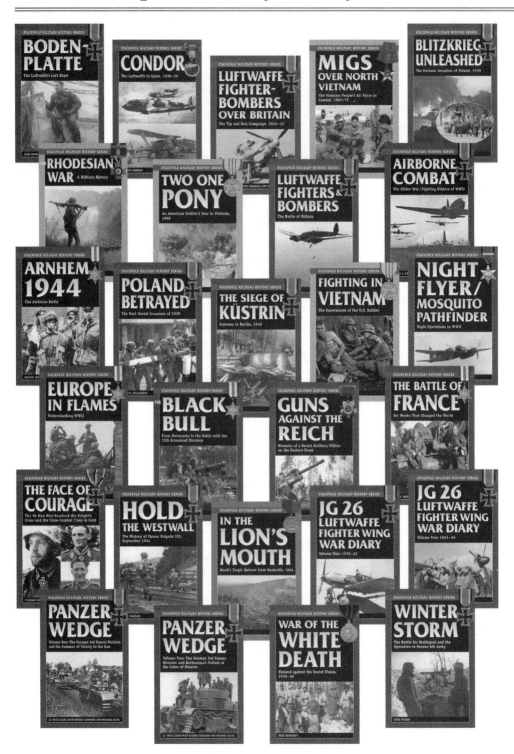

Real battles. Real soldiers. Real stories.

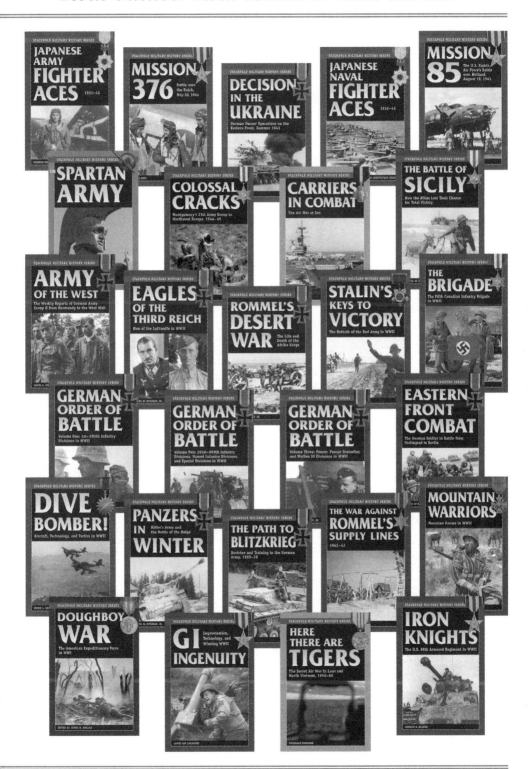

Stackpole Military History Series

Real battles. Real soldiers. Real stories.

Stackpole Military History Series

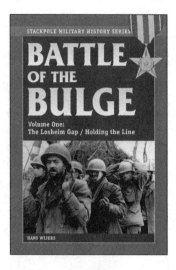

BATTLE OF THE BULGE
VOLUME ONE: THE LOSHEIM GAP /
HOLDING THE LINE
Hans Wijers

Most accounts of the Battle of the Bulge focus on the
center, where the 101st Airborne held Bastogne, but
the Germans' main thrust actually occurred to the
north, where Sepp Dietrich's 6th SS Panzer Army
stormed through the Losheim Gap on its way to Liege
and Antwerp. In this region of thick forests, snowy
fields, and muddy trails during the battle's first week in
December 1944, U.S. troops from the 2nd and 99th
Infantry Divisions successfully halted the best of the
German war machine, including the 12th SS Panzer
and the 3rd Fallschirmjäger Divisions.

Paperback • 6 x 9 • 448 pages • 177 b/w photos

WWW.STACKPOLEBOOKS.COM
1-800-732-3669

Stackpole Military History Series

BATTLE OF THE BULGE

VOLUME TWO: HELL AT BÜTGENBACH / SEIZE THE BRIDGES

Hans Wijers

During the first week of the Battle of the Bulge, the Germans'
6th SS Panzer Army rolled down the road to Bütgenbach,
where the 26th Infantry Regiment of the U.S. 1st Infantry
Division held out against constant attacks at the southern end
of Elsenborn Ridge. Meanwhile, Jochen Peiper's SS battle
group raced toward the critical river bridges at Stavelot and
Trois Ponts, massacring American prisoners along the way
near Malmedy. The U.S 30th Infantry Division and other units
put up stiff resistance, destroyed the bridges, and forced
Peiper's men to withdraw.

Paperback • 6 x 9 • 352 pages • 185 b/w photos

WWW.STACKPOLEBOOKS.COM
1-800-732-3669

Stackpole Military History Series

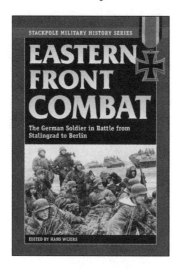

EASTERN FRONT COMBAT
THE GERMAN SOLDIER IN BATTLE FROM
STALINGRAD TO BERLIN
Edited by Hans Wijers

In these firsthand accounts—never before published in English—German soldiers describe the horrors of combat on the Eastern Front during World War II. A panzer crewman holds out to the bitter end at Stalingrad, fighting the Soviets as well as cold and hunger. An assault gun commander seeks out and destroys enemy tanks in Poland. Along the Oder River, a ragtag antiaircraft battery turns its guns against Russian infantry. And in Berlin a paratrooper makes a last, desperate stand in the war's closing days.

Paperback • 6 x 9 • 336 pages • 109 photos, 4 maps

WWW.STACKPOLEBOOKS.COM
1-800-732-3669

Stackpole Military History Series

THE KEY TO THE BULGE
THE BATTLE FOR LOSHEIMERGRABEN
Stephen M. Rusiecki

On December 16, 1944, when Hitler launched a surprise attack in the Ardennes to start the Battle of the Bulge, the green U.S. 394th Infantry Regiment of the 99th Infantry Division occupied a critical road junction at Losheimergraben, Belgium. For thirty-six hours, the 394th defended the crossroads against repeated assaults by crack forces of the Sixth SS Panzer Army, which represented the main effort of the German offensive. By the time the regiment finally withdrew, the Germans had suffered a delay from which they could not recover.

Paperback • 6 x 9 • 240 pages • 24 b/w photos, 6 maps

WWW.STACKPOLEBOOKS.COM
1-800-732-3669

Stackpole Military History Series

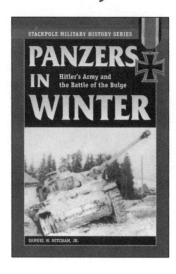

PANZERS IN WINTER
HITLER'S ARMY AND THE BATTLE OF THE BULGE
Samuel W. Mitcham, Jr.

Before dawn on December 16, 1944, German forces rolled through the frozen Ardennes in their last major offensive in the west, thus starting the Battle of the Bulge, which would become the U.S. Army's bloodiest engagement of World War II. Catching the Allies by surprise, the Germans made early gains, demolished the inexperienced U.S. 106th Infantry Division, and fought hard, but American counterattacks—and tenacious resistance in towns like Bastogne—combined with mounting German casualties and fuel shortages to force the German Army into a retreat from which it never recovered.

Paperback • 6 x 9 • 240 pages • 27 b/w photos, 14 maps

WWW.STACKPOLEBOOKS.COM
1-800-732-3669

Stackpole Military History Series

BEYOND THE BEACHHEAD
THE 29TH INFANTRY DIVISION IN NORMANDY
Joseph Balkoski

Previously untested in battle, the American 29th
Infantry Division stormed Omaha Beach on D-Day and
began a summer of bloody combat in the hedgerows
of Normandy. Against a tenacious German foe, the
division fought fiercely for every inch of ground and,
at great cost, liberated the town of St. Lô. This new
and expanded edition of Joseph Balkoski's classic
follows the 29th through the final stages of the
campaign and the brutal struggle for the town of Vire.

Paperback • 6 x 9 • 352 pages • 36 b/w photos, 30 maps

WWW.STACKPOLEBOOKS.COM
1-800-732-3669

Stackpole Military History Series

TIGERS IN THE MUD
THE COMBAT CAREER OF GERMAN PANZER
COMMANDER OTTO CARIUS

Otto Carius,
translated by Robert J. Edwards

World War II began with a metallic roar as the
German Blitzkrieg raced across Europe, spearheaded
by the most dreadful weapon of the twentieth century:
the Panzer. Tank commander Otto Carius thrusts the
reader into the thick of battle, replete with the
blood, smoke, mud, and gunpowder so common
to the elite German fighting units.

Paperback • 6 x 9 • 368 pages
51 photos, 48 illustrations, 3 maps

WWW.STACKPOLEBOOKS.COM
1-800-732-3669

Stackpole Military History Series

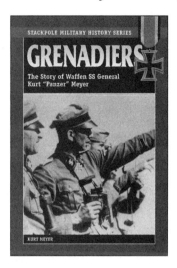

GRENADIERS
THE STORY OF WAFFEN SS GENERAL
KURT "PANZER" MEYER

Kurt Meyer

Known for his bold and aggressive leadership, Kurt
Meyer was one of the most highly decorated German
soldiers of World War II. As commander of various
units, from a motorcycle company to the Hitler Youth
Panzer Division, he saw intense combat across Europe,
from the invasion of Poland in 1939 to the 1944
campaign for Normandy, where he fell into Allied
hands and was charged with war crimes.

Paperback • 6 x 9 • 448 pages • 93 b/w photos

WWW.STACKPOLEBOOKS.COM
1-800-732-3669

Stackpole Military History Series

PANZER ACES
GERMAN TANK COMMANDERS OF WORLD WAR II
Franz Kurowski

With the order "Panzers forward!" German tanks
rolled into battle, smashing into the enemy with
engines roaring and muzzles flashing. From Poland
and the Eastern Front to the Ardennes, Italy, and
northern Africa, panzers stunned their opponents—
and the world—with their lightning speed and raw
power, and the soldiers, like Michael, who manned
these lethal machines were among the
boldest and most feared of World War II.

Paperback • 6 x 9 • 480 pages • 60 b/w photos

WWW.STACKPOLEBOOKS.COM
1-800-732-3669

Stackpole Military History Series

INFANTRY ACES
THE GERMAN SOLDIER IN COMBAT IN WORLD WAR II
Franz Kurowski

This is an authentic account of German infantry aces—one paratrooper, two members of the Waffen-SS, and five Wehrmacht soldiers—who were thrust into the maelstrom of death and destruction that was World War II. Enduring countless horrors on the icy Eastern Front, in the deserts of Africa, and on other bloody fields, these rank-and-file soldiers took on enemy units alone, battled giant tanks, stormed hills, and rescued wounded comrades.

Paperback • 6 x 9 • 512 pages • 43 b/w photos, 11 maps

WWW.STACKPOLEBOOKS.COM
1-800-732-3669

Stackpole Military History Series

LUFTWAFFE ACES
GERMAN COMBAT PILOTS OF WORLD WAR II
Franz Kurowski,
translated by David Johnston

Whether providing close-support for the blitzkrieg, bombing enemy cities and industrial centers, or attacking Allied fighters and bombers during both day and night, the Luftwaffe played a critical role in World War II and saw some of the most harrowing combat of the war. Franz Kurowski puts readers in the cockpit with seven of Germany's deadliest and most successful pilots.

Paperback • 6 x 9 • 400 pages • 73 b/w photos

WWW.STACKPOLEBOOKS.COM
1-800-732-3669

Stackpole Military History Series

ARMOR BATTLES
OF THE WAFFEN-SS
1943–45

Will Fey, translated by Henri Henschler

The Waffen-SS were considered the elite of the
German armed forces in the Second World War and
were involved in almost continuous combat. From
the sweeping tank battle of Kursk on the Russian
front to the bitter fighting among the hedgerows
of Normandy and the offensive in the Ardennes,
these men and their tanks made history.

Paperback • 6 x 9 • 384 pages • 32 photos, 15 drawings, 4 maps

WWW.STACKPOLEBOOKS.COM
1-800-732-3669

Stackpole Military History Series

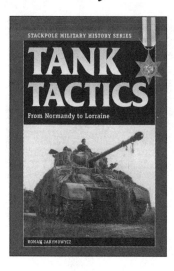

TANK TACTICS
FROM NORMANDY TO LORRAINE
Roman Jarymowycz

Roman Jarymowycz draws on after-action reports, war diaries, and other primary sources to examine the tactical ideas underpinning World War II tank warfare as conducted by Allied commanders in France from July to September 1944. His study focuses on Operation Goodwood, Montgomery's attack near Caen; Operations Cobra and Spring, the Normandy breakout by Bradley's U.S. First Army and the Canadians' simultaneous assault to the east; Operation Totalize, the effort to break through German defenses south of Caen; Operation Tractable, the Canadian and Polish attempt to capture Falaise; and Patton's September battles in Lorraine.

Paperback • 6 x 9 • 384 pages
10 b/w photos, 14 maps, 19 diagrams

WWW.STACKPOLEBOOKS.COM
1-800-732-3669

Stackpole Military History Series

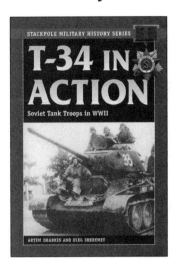

T-34 IN ACTION
SOVIET TANK TROOPS IN WORLD WAR II
Artem Drabkin and Oleg Sheremet

Regarded by many as the best tank of World War II, the Soviet T-34 was fast, well-armored, and heavily gunned—more than a match for the German panzers. From Moscow to Kiev, Leningrad to Stalingrad, Kursk to Berlin, T-34s rumbled through the dust, mud, and snow of the Eastern Front and propelled the Red Army to victory. These firsthand accounts from Soviet tankmen evoke the harrowing conditions they faced: the dirt and grime of battlefield life, the claustrophobia inside a tank, the thick smoke and deafening blasts of combat, and the bloody aftermath.

Paperback • 6 x 9 • 208 pages • 40 photos, 5 maps

WWW.STACKPOLEBOOKS.COM
1-800-732-3669

Also available from Stackpole Books

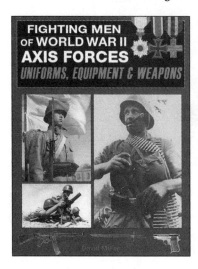
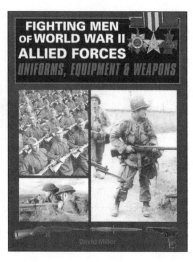

FIGHTING MEN OF WORLD WAR II
VOLUME 1: AXIS FORCES
VOLUME 2: ALLIED FORCES
David Miller

These comprehensive volumes present a full-color
look at Axis and Allied soldiers in World War II,
covering their weapons, equipment, clothing,
rations, and more. The Axis volume includes Germany,
Italy, and Japan while the Allied volume presents
troops from the United States, Great Britain, and the
Soviet Union. These books create a vivid picture of
the daily life and battle conditions of the fighting
men of the Second World War.

Hardcover • 9 x 12 • 384 pages • 600 color illustrations

WWW.STACKPOLEBOOKS.COM
1-800-732-3669